A CITY
ON A MOUNTAIN

PADRE PIO OF PIETRELCINA,
O.F.M. CAP.

By

Pascal P. Parente, S.T.D., Ph.D., J.C.B.

PROFESSOR OF ASCETICAL AND MYSTICAL THEOLOGY
AT THE CATHOLIC UNIVERSITY OF AMERICA

Ave Maria Institute
Washington, New Jersey

Nihil Obstat
WILLIAM A. MARGERUM, S.T.D.
Censor Librorum

Imprimatur:
✠ GEORGE W. AHR, S.T.D.
Bishop of Trenton

N.B. The Imprimatur implies nothing more than that the
material contained herein has been examined by the
Diocesan Censor and that nothing contrary to faith or
morals has been found therein.

ISBN 0-911988-35-1

In obedience to the decree of Pope Urban VIII, the
author declares that the graces and other supernatural
facts related in this book rest on human authority
alone, and he submits himself without reserve to the
decisions of the Apostolic See.

CONTENTS

iii

INTRODUCTION

"A city seated on a mountain cannot be hid" (Matt. 5: 14). It is seen from the land, from the sea, from the sky. Low-hanging clouds and rising mist often hide it from view, but when the clouds lift in the late hours of the afternoon and the haze vanishes, the city on the mountain is seen again—transfigured and all aflame, like a reflecting mirror in the golden rays of the setting sun.

The story of Padre Pio of Pietrelcina is like the story of a city on a mountain. He, too, was under a cloud for a number of years. His gifts, even his virtue, were under suspicion. The theory of hysteria, which for some people should explain everything, but actually proves nothing, was offered as the cause of his stigmata. The sponsor of that theory, in our case, is now dead; so is his theory.

With the above words Father Pascal Parente, one of the greatest living experts on mystical theology, opened this book on the most famous mystic of our century: Padre Pio.

This book was written while Father Parente was still professor of Theology at the Catholic University of America. It has become a classic.

After Padre Pio's death on Sept. 23rd, 1968, the publishers thought to "update" this book which had been written when the famous Padre was still alive. But nothing of importance in Padre Pio's life is missing from these pages except some of the more extraordinary miracles attributed to him in the last years of his life.

A group of members of the Blue Army of Our Lady

iv

of Fatima went on a special trip from the United States to Italy in September of 1968 for the fiftieth anniversary of the Padre's stigmata. On September 17th they had Mass at Assisi. It was the Feast of the stigmata of Saint Francis. The following day (Sept. 18th) they had Mass in the Holy House of Nazareth, at Loreto, where Father Pio all during his life had sent most difficult cases of possession. For the exorcisms, Father Pio often became present in the Holy House by bilocation.

On Sept. 19th, the group arrived in San Giovanni for one of the biggest days in Padre Pio's history: the fiftieth anniversary of the stigmata. His devotees had come from all over the world. And the Bishop of the Diocese, who had previously taken a neutral stand on the Padre, was there to bless the crypt where one day Padre Pio would be buried. It was the "golden jubilee" of a living crucifix.

By some inscrutable action of Providence, this American group was the last ever to have an audience with Padre Pio. It was then recalled that several years before Father Pio had predicted: "Russia will be converted when there is a Blue Army member for every Communist." And he had accepted all who sign the Blue Army pledge as his "spiritual children", provided they lived up to the pledge.

This illustrated biography of the "Living Crucifix" known as Padre Pio is timeless.

Father Pio is the only priest in history known to have borne in his body the five wounds... like those carried by St. Francis of Assisi. And he lived in our midst, suffering and bleeding for half a century, as a consolation to those who are tempted to despair and as a warning to those who are presumptuous.

There are many books about Padre Pio. There will be many more. But this particular book was "before its time" and is one of the finest, condensed views of Father Pio AS a living crucifix. Dr. Parente, author of the book (and himself now gone to his eternal reward), was one of the few great experts of our time on mystical theology. He came to know Father Pio because of his STUDY of the phenomenon of what is known as stigmatization. And yet he did not write a ponderous book dwelling mainly on the phenomenon itself. Like everyone who came to know Father Pio, Dr. Parente was touched by the mission of holiness which flowed from Father Pio like a wave of Grace. Father Pio was Christ's gift to our day. Father Pio was an assertion of the reality of Christ in our world, especially in the Eucharistic liturgy. His wave of Grace came from Christ through the "Lady of Graces"... to whom Father Pio attributed all, and to whom he sent all who sought to find her Divine Son.

How could any author present an adequate portrait of such an important, living message to the twentieth century?

Dr. Parente did. And when he died he left the book to the Blue Army, whose members Father Pio had adopted as "his special children", meaning that he promised to pray FOR EACH ONE, individually and by name, every day. If he could make that promise while he was on earth, how much more must he not be honoring it now!

No book after this one by Dr. Parente will have a greater ring of authority. It details many of Padre Pio's miracles (such as cures of cancer, bilocation, perfume, conversions) and was published long before Padre Pio's death, when any mistakes or errors would have been corrected. It was on sale in San Giovanni, in Mr. Abresch's store, for over a decade! And Mr. Abresch gave Father Parente the photographs and is himself one whose miraculous conversion is described in these pages.

Chapter One

Winter and Springtime at Our Lady of Grace

IT was a cold evening in mid-December of the year 1917 when a frail young Capuchin friar knocked at the door of the Monastery of Our Lady of Grace in San Giovanni Rotondo. Recently dismissed from the army because of pulmonary tuberculosis, he had been assigned to convalesce in this monastery by his religious superiors. His military uniform had been discarded at his home in Pietrelcina, and there he had garbed himself once again in the brown Capuchin habit and sandals he loved so well.

As the newcomer waited for the old and smiling Brother Costantino to open the door, he turned eastward for a last look at the vast and beautiful panorama before him—a sweep of land from the Gargano mountains to the Adriatic and the Gulf of Manfredonia. Cold north winds were blowing against his tunic and biting at his bare feet. Then suddenly the door opened.

"Praised be Jesus Christ!" said Brother Costantino, holding the heavy door against the mounting gale. "Come in, Padre Pio. I'll show you to the cell that Father Guardian wants you to occupy. This way, please."

Two flights of steps to the second floor, then down a long corridor until they reached Cell Five. Here the Brother stopped and waited for Padre Pio to finish reading the words written above the door: *"The Glory of the World Hath Always Sadness*

1

for a Companion." Then he asked for the priestly blessing and returned to his work.

Glory has now come to Cell Five, although not the glory of this world. Suffering, agony and crucifixion have marked that poor little room since Padre Pio entered it on that long ago December evening. But sadness has not come, except perhaps the sadness of Gethsemani. People from many parts of the world and from all walks of life have stood within its walls, but the plain little cell is still the same in its poverty and simplicity. Yet in one sense it *is* richer, for now it has become an oasis of peace and of comfort for all who visit it in a spirit of humility and faith.

When Padre Pio arrived at the Monastery of Our Lady of Grace in December, 1917, with a diagnosis of tuberculosis, his superiors were all but convinced that he would live only a short time—perhaps until the almond trees began to bloom in the valley; at the most, until the vineyards turned crimson and gold in the fall. Poor Padre—so kind, so good—to die so young!

But when the almond trees, the cherry trees and all the other trees were a symphony of color in the spring of 1918, Padre Pio was still occupying Cell Five. Then one day he was seen going back and forth through the monastery as if in a trance.

"Where has Jesus gone?" he kept asking everyone he met.

The Brothers looked at him uneasily, then at one another, and finally Brother Nicola shook his head.

"Poor Padre, he's lost his mind," he declared.

The good Brothers had never read, or did not remember,

---

* *All the illustrations in this book are published with the kind permission of Signor Frederico Abresch of San Giovanni Rotondo (Foggia), Italy, who took the original photographs.*

these words from Holy Scripture: "I sought him, and found him not: I called, and he did not answer me. . . . I adjure you, O daughters of Jerusalem, if you find my beloved, that you tell him that I languish with love."[1]

Through a miracle of grace, a mystical springtime in the soul of Padre Pio was beginning to bring new life and energy to his frail body, so that soon that body began to blossom, too. Yes, in the fall of 1918, five crimson "roses" appeared on the body of the young Capuchin, one on each of his hands and feet, and one on his left side just under his heart. They were the stigmata, the living wounds of Christ Crucified, but we have called them roses because of their color and their fragrance which is sweeter than all the flowers of spring.

Others, though, have called them hysterical marks, necrobiosis, a natural manifestation or phenomenon. But they are still there today, over forty years later, still bleeding, still fragrant, and Padre Pio is no longer the frail man afflicted with tuberculosis, but a strong, hard-working, healthy person, an instrument of grace for many who have met him or have been recommended to his prayers.

It is not our intention to express an opinion on the nature of the phenomena in the life of Padre Pio. This belongs to the supreme Authority of the Church. The Church does not canonize any living person, no matter how holy that person may be. In her eternal mission, she is not swayed by the enthusiasm and the admiration of the crowds. She waits patiently for God's own time, because both justice and truth shine forth more brilliantly when all the clouds of popular enthusiasm have passed away.

In the present account of Padre Pio's life, we shall limit our-

---

[1] Canticle of Canticles, 5: 6 f.

CAPUCHIN MONASTERY AND CHURCH OF OUR LADY OF GRACE.

ZI' ORAZIO
PADRE PIO'S FATHER.

ZI' GIUSEPPA
PADRE PIO'S MOTHER.

selves to a presentation of the facts we have gathered from various sources and from personal knowledge. If opinions favorable to Padre Pio are expressed in these pages, they should be regarded merely as personal impressions. The story of Padre Pio's life is eminently the story of his soul. At present we can catch only a reflex here and there of that life, his inner life, in which alone one can find the explanation of the extraordinary facts we are going to present.

Naturally we have followed with great interest all obtainable information regarding Padre Pio; and with no less interest we have watched the attitude of the Church in his case. First, silent and prudent waiting; then, a declaration of the Holy Office warning the faithful to abstain from visiting Padre Pio and from writing to him. (This stage will be especially examined later in this book.)

For a while the controversy over Padre Pio developed into a violent persecution, and for about two years (1930-32) he was not allowed to say Mass in public or to hear confessions. To some people this meant a total condemnation of Padre Pio. But it was not so. When the Archbishop of Manfredonia (in whose diocese San Giovanni Rotondo lies), reported on Padre Pio to Pope Pius XI, the Holy Father said to him: "I was not unfavorably inclined (towards Padre Pio) but badly informed."[2] After this, the holy friar was once again permitted to say Mass publicly and to hear confessions.

Pope Pius XII is well disposed towards Padre Pio. Since the fall of 1939 he has been seen occasionally outside the monastery. The Sunday edition of *Osservatore Romano,* February 22, 1948, published a letter by R. S. of Aversa with the following comment:

---

[2] "Non ero maldisposto, ma malinformato."

"There is no longer any prohibition to visit Padre Pio of Pietrelcina or to write to him."

Today the humble friar appears greater than ever, after so many years of persecution and misunderstanding. Humility and obedience are the real tests of Christian virtue, and Padre Pio has passed both tests with admirable success*

"The glory of the world hath always sadness for a companion." But not the glory that comes from the testimony of a good conscience. There was no sadness in Cell Five during all those years of seclusion. It was one of the few places on earth where one could find that "perfect joy" of which Saint Francis of Assisi spoke to Brother Leo seven centuries ago:

"Now hear the end of all this, Brother Leo! More than all grace and all the gifts of the Holy Ghost, which Christ vouchsafes to His friends, is the conquering of yourself and the willing endurance of contempt, injustice, suffering and harshness."[3]

---

[3] *Fioretti,* 9.

*It must be kept in mind that when Dr. Parente wrote this biography Father Pio was living. Like St. Francis, the venerable father was in a sense "canonized" while he was still living.

Chapter Two

The Young Francis Forgione

PADRE PIO was born in Pietrelcina, a town of some four thousand inhabitants, a few miles north of the city of Benevento in southern Italy, on May 25, 1887, at five o'clock in the afternoon. He was baptized the following day in the parish church of Saint Mary of the Angels and named Francesco in honor of Saint Francis of Assisi. His father, Orazio Forgione, and his mother, Maria Giuseppa de Nunzio, were poor, illiterate farmers, but possessed of deep Christian faith, simplicity and honesty. Besides Francesco they had another son, Michael, and three daughters. One of the girls, Grace, became a nun in the Convent of Saint Bridget in Rome, taking the name of Sister Pia some time after her brother Francis had changed his own name to that of Fra Pio by entering the Capuchin novitiate.

Little is known about young Francis Forgione's early years, and that little was learned chiefly from Zi' Orazio,[1] his father. (Padre Pio is extremely reserved and uncommunicative about his past.)

The Forgione family owned a poor little two-room house in a narrow street, close to the old castle which dominates the whole town and surrounding valleys. Not far from his home, young Francis used to watch the other children playing in the

---

[1] Zi', for *zio*, uncle, and for *zia*, aunt, is a colloquial prefix for elderly persons among country people in south and central Italy.

little square before an ancient church dedicated to Saint Pius V. Yet the lad's great attraction was not playing, but praying. Only five years old, he had already promised Saint Francis of Assisi that he would imitate his example and some day be one of his family. The unfailing sweetness, obedience and humility of the little boy so inspired his father that he left no stone unturned to assist him attain a vocation which was even then manifest; to become a *monaco da Messa*—a religious priest.

His mother was related to the Archpriest Don Salvatore Pannullo, the local pastor. She was such a devout Christian that, regardless of the great amount of work to be done in the fields or at home, she would always find time to attend daily Mass. Don Salvatore (known as Zi' Tore to the Forgione family), took a great liking to little Francis. With true fatherly interest, he set about forming his character and guiding his innocent soul towards the luminous goal he had chosen so early in life, that of being a priest of God in the spirit of Saint Francis. (Years later he was to become the first confidant of the mysterious work of divine grace in Padre Pio's soul, and a sure guide in the bitter struggle against the forces of evil unleashed against the young Levite.)

The Forgiones owned a couple of acres of land not far from Pietrelcina which they cultivated most diligently—the little farm being their main source of sustenance. But despite their best efforts, there were never ten *lire* (two dollars, in those days) in Zi' Orazio's home at one time. In the words of Padre Pio:

"We had little. But, thank God, we never lacked anything."

However, the whole family was satisfied with their humble lot, and young Francis even found ways of secretly depriving himself of food and drink in a spirit of mortification. Indeed, he was scarcely nine years old when his mother discovered that he had been sleeping on the bare floor with a stone for a pillow for quite some time.

Francis attended the local public school, from which he graduated at the age of ten. When not at school, he tended sheep for his father and brother on the little farm, or did odd chores at home for his mother. In the evening he would join the young boys of the neighborhood in the little square before Saint Pius' church.

Those radiant hours of sunset in southern Italy were enchanting beyond words. Looking west from Pietrelcina, the boys could see beautiful Mount Taburnus, known as the sleeping beauty of Samnium, rising solemn and silent against the sky. To the south, they could feast their eyes on the majestic Neapolitan Apennines, particularly on Mount Partenio. And here, in this lovely and peaceful setting, they played and sang and were happy. But if there was any profanity, or even a simple falsehood, young Francis would suddenly turn pale as if personally hurt. Tears would come to his eyes and he would walk quietly home or to the church to pray.

It was perhaps on account of such an attitude that Padre Pio once remarked that as a boy he had been a *maccherone senza sale,* a local idiom for an apathetic fellow. He loved solitude, but was never averse to innocent diversions, or to singing and playing. Since Pietrelcina boasted a concert band, well-known and appreciated in neighboring towns for its extensive repertoire and fine performance, Francis' young soul often found its way to God on the wings of sweet harmonies from Verdi, Donizzetti or Rossini.

"Pietrelcina," writes a convert and disciple of Padre Pio, "is the home of pious creatures, the country of ardent souls ... of good-natured, simple-minded people, nursing inexpressible poetical feelings in their hearts. In this mountain countryside, a poet could draw inspiration enabling him to sing the noblest song in life."[2]

Pietrelcina and neighboring towns, with Benevento as their center, represent home to an old and hardy race—the stubborn highlanders known to history as Samnites. For half a century these fought bravely and fiercely against the invading Roman legions, and in 321 B.C. humbled them with ignominious terms, compelling them to pass man by man "under the yoke" at a mountain pass called the Caudine Forks. Yet, strangely enough, the liberty-loving Samnites were among the first people in Italy to surrender freely to the yoke of Christ. They accepted the Faith as early as the year 40 A.D., when the first Church was founded by the disciples of Christ in the city of Benevento. Padre Pio is in every respect a true son of these people who, all through the centuries, have kept the Faith unblemished.

After his graduation from grammar school in 1897, young Francis was placed under the instruction of a private teacher. This was a retired priest of the town, Don Domenico Tizzani by name, who gave the youngster the equivalent of a junior high school education, with special emphasis on Latin. In the meantime, the little family of Zi' Orazio had been growing. This fact, and the added expenses for Francis' teacher and books, strained the very modest family resources beyond the limit. In 1898, encouraged by the example of friends and neighbors, Zi' Orazio finally decided to emigrate to America. Here he would be able to secure better wages and so assist his faithful Giuseppa in bringing up the family and in defraying the expenses of young Francis' studies for the priesthood.

---

[2] From Doubt to Faith, by A. Del Fante, p. 38.

After two years of work with Don Tizzani, Francis was given a more efficient teacher in the person of Professor Angelo Caccavo. He remained with him until the summer of 1902. Then, in the fall of that year, he applied for and was admitted to the Order of the Capuchins of the Province of Foggia and was assigned to the novitiate at Morcone, which he entered during November of that same year.

The boy's vocation to be a Franciscan had always remained clear and firm in his mind. Asked one day why he had chosen to enter the Capuchins, he smiled and said: "I always liked bearded religious!"

FRANCIS FORGIONE (PADRE PIO) 14 YEARS OLD

Chapter Three

Capuchin Novice and Student

THE Capuchins are the most recent of the three independent branches of the Franciscan Order. They were founded by Blessed Matteo da Bascio in 1525 for the purpose of restoring a literal observance of the rule of Saint Francis of Assisi. The friars wear a brown habit girded with a white cord, a long pointed hood (the Italian *cappuccio*), sandals and a beard.* They are a mendicant Order whose lay Brothers go on begging tours for the community. The mode of life, based on the rule of Saint Francis, is simple and austere, yet happy and cheerful.

After a few weeks in the Monastery at Morcone, young Francis was finally granted the livery of Saint Francis, the Capuchin garb. In putting on the new man he dropped his baptismal name, as is customary in most religious communities, and became Fra Pio (Brother Pius.) The family name of Forgione was also replaced by the name of his birthplace, so that henceforth the young novice would be known as Fra Pio of Pietrelcina.

We do not know why the name of Pius was given to Francis by his superiors, but we cannot help thinking that it was a providential choice. On August 4 of that same year, 1903, Giuseppe Sarto assumed the name of Pius on his election as Pope, and for the next eleven years he governed the Church as Pius X. Today we venerate him as St. Pius X. After a short interval another Pius sat on the chair of Saint Peter—Pius XI, 1922-1939—who was followed immediately by another great Pope of the

* The beard is now optional.

same name, our present gloriously reigning Pius XII. We may say, therefore, that the name of Pius has ruled the world of the spirit during the first half of the twentieth century.

At some distance from the majesty of the Vatican, another Pius has played his spiritual role (in a much humbler measure, of course) by means of prayer, suffering, obedience and special gifts of grace. His name is Padre Pio, and he has carried that name with honor for the last forty-nine years.

With the reception of the religious habit on January 22, 1903, Fra Pio started his canonical year of novitiate. This was a time of probation—the community testing the fitness of the novice, the novice testing his own aptitude for the new life. It was a year of adaptation and spiritual formation, of learning the rule and living it. Fra Pio entered upon the experience with a zestful enthusiasm all his own.

In the fall of 1903, Zi' Orazio returned from America. After a reunion with his family in Pietrelcina, he hastened to pay a visit to Fra Pio, accompanied by his wife. The two remained a few days in Morcone and were allowed to see their son in the presence of the Novice Master. But their joy was greatly lessened by reason of the boy's appearance. He was extremely emaciated and pale, his eyes generally fixed upon the floor during the various conversations.

Zi' Orazio went straight to the Father Guardian. "What have you done to my boy?" he demanded anxiously. "Why, I scarcely recognize him!"

The good old man felt he ought to take his son home, but the Guardian reassured him. There was nothing wrong with Fra Pio. When he had learned to moderate his mortifications, he would be quite himself again.

Soon after this visit from his parents, Fra Pio was transferred to the Monastery of Saint Elia a Pianisi (Campobasso) where on January 22, 1904, he completed his novitiate and made his religious Profession.

The following six years were devoted to study and preparation for the priesthood. Fra Pio had to integrate and complete the classical courses, then take philosophy and theology. He carried the same diligence and application to the formation of his mind that had been his in the formation of the heart. In particular, the study of sacred theology was approached with deep interest and devotion, and his superiors often found him working at his lessons on his knees, his mind lost in the contemplation of the mysteries contained in the text.

Theology was actually a meditation for Fra Pio, meditation in which not only the mind but also the heart and the emotions took part. This fact may partially explain the extraordinary effect that his words have had in later life.

"This priest does not say anything different or unusual, yet the effect on the soul is so different and so unusual!"

Such is the reaction of many of Padre Pio's converts, who have tried to analyze the mysterious process of the sudden change that has taken place within themselves.

There was no let-up in Fra Pio's mortifications during this period. If he ever failed in this respect, it was only by excess, as when in the Monastery of Venafro he spent three weeks without touching any food except Holy Communion, yet neglected none of his customary duties.

We find the young Capuchin in various houses of his Province during these six years: at Saint Elia Pianisi, Venafro, Saint Marco, Montefusco. Because of his frail health, he was often sent home during the summer months for a little vacation with his relatives in Pietrelcina. He would suddenly get sick to an alarming degree during these years, then just as suddenly recover his strength.

"One day the friars sent for me," says Zi' Orazio, "and when I arrived at the monastery, a certain Brother was waiting for me.

" 'How is Fra Pio?' I asked.

" 'Ah, Zi' Orazio, he hasn't touched any food for fourteen days! We are all weeping for fear that he may never be able to walk again. If you wish, take him home, but be careful to keep the dishes and the silver he uses away from the rest of the family, especially if you have young children.' " (They feared that he had tuberculosis.)

"Well, if he must die, he shall die at home," said Zi' Orazio sadly.

Having obtained the necessary permission, father and son made themselves ready for the trip home. But by now Fra Pio was so weak that two friars had to assist him with dressing and walking.

"What shall I do?" thought Zi' Orazio. "He may die on the way!"

They reached the railroad station in the company of two other friars who had been riding with them in a coach. Zi' Orazio turned anxiously to his son: "Fra Pio, how do you feel now?" he asked.

"A little better," was the reply.

The poor old man, who had crossed the ocean via steerage, had no interest in economy where his boy was concerned. He bought first-class tickets for the trip home and insisted that Fra Pio have some good wine. But the young man refused. However, as soon as he reached home, he showed a surprising interest in food.

"Mother, what have you got for supper?" he demanded eagerly.

"Turnips, son."

"Fine! They're my favorite dish."

And at table that evening he ate for three! He was cured![1]

It was now early in the spring of 1910. The few savings which Zi' Orazio had brought from America had long since vanished. One March day he went to Fra Pio and announced that he was off for the United States again.

"I'm leaving tonight," he said.

"All right, Dad," replied Fra Pio, "but this is the last time we let you cross the ocean; you must never try it again." And Zi' Orazio left home for America almost on the eve of his son's Ordination to the priesthood. He lived in Jamaica, N.Y.

From Pietrelcina, Fra Pio returned to the Monastery of Montefusco to join his classmates who were about to conclude their theological studies. The new norms issued by Pope Pius X made it mandatory for religious theological students to pass their final examination in the presence of the local Bishop. Preparations for the great event had already been made, and one morning all the students boarded an improvised wagon to drive to Benevento for their examination. However, when the Rector saw Fra Pio among them, he shook his head.

"Not you, Piuccio,"[2] he said kindly. "You've been sick, and the trip will be too much for you."

However, Fra Pio had other ideas. "I'll make it, Father Rector even if I have to *walk* to Benevento," he declared earnestly.

He did go, and received the highest grades of the whole class.

---

[1] This charming episode is one of the many narrated by Zi' Orazio himself, with an abundance of particulars, and reported by L. Patri in his *Cenni Biografici su Padre Pio da Pietrelcina*, P. 21 ff.

[2] An endearing diminutive for Pio.

Chapter Four

The Priest

THE realization of a cherished dream is always a source of joy. For Fra Pio, this realization took place on the morning of August 10, 1910, in the Cathedral of Benevento, when he was ordained a priest. A younger Capuchin asked him then whether he had slept well the night before.

"How could I sleep, with my heart bursting with joy?" was the touching reply.

The next day, August 11, Padre Pio said a Low Mass in Pietrelcina. This was on a Thursday. The following Sunday, August 14, he sang his first High Mass in the Church of Saint Mary of the Angels, where he had been baptized twenty-three years before.[1]

In such fashion did Francis Forgione begin his priestly career. There were celebrations at Pietrelcina in which almost the entire population took part. And in far-off America, Zi' Orazio and his fellow-immigrants also had a little party of their own to celebrate the great day.

It is difficult to describe the holy joy which fills the heart of a young priest when, for the first time, the Son of God becomes present in his hands under the form of bread and wine. Padre Pio's feelings on this occasion may be surmised from the few

---

[1] Practically all the books on Padre Pio give the date of May 10, 1910, as that of his Ordination, but this is incorrect. Also, the first Mass was said at Pietrelcina, not at Benevento.

lines he wrote on the holy pictures that were distributed on the Silver Jubilee of his Ordination in 1935:

"O Jesus, my Victim and my Love! In the joy of these renewed raptures make of me an altar for Thy Holy Cross, a golden chalice for Thy Blood, holocaust, love, prayer for myself and my dear ones, another Jesus for all the spiritual children near and far."

The realization of his first dream was only a symbol of things to come. To be another Jesus, a victim, a holocaust, was his second dream. In 1935, when he wrote the foregoing words, he had already realized this second dream. He had the five living wounds of Christ in his own body and because of them had been condemned and persecuted. This was his Calvary. But now, in 1910, he had yet to tread the Way of the Cross.

Once the Ordination festivities at home were over, Padre Pio returned to his religious community. Here he was seized by the mysterious hyperthermiae (unusually high fevers) which he had suffered as a student. Accordingly the superiors decided to send him back to his native town for recovery, where he remained for some five or six years.

At this time the spiritual life of Padre Pio was a secret known only to God and to his director. However, one thing seemed to betray the young priest even in those early years—his Mass. Never before had people seen such devotion at the altar. Never before had the drama of Calvary been enacted so vividly before their eyes. Naturally everyone was edified by such piety, although eventually some did complain to the pastor, Don Salvatore Pannullo, about the duration of Padre Pio's Mass—an hour and one-half! In fact, several times during the Holy Sacrifice the young friar would be lost in ecstasy. And he would have continued in this mystical state had not Don Salvatore

NEW HOMES ALONG THE ROAD LEADING TO THE CAPUCHIN MONASTERY. IN THE DISTANCE, TO THE RIGHT, IS THE TOWN OF SAN GIOVANNI ROTONDO.

23

(his pastor and confessor) hit upon the practical solution of giving him a mental command and ringing a little bell in order to recall him to the performance of his sacred duties. (These same ecstatic seizures would occur during his prayers of thanksgiving after Mass.)

One day when Padre Pio did not return home for dinner, his mother, seeing the sexton coming her way, could not control her anxiety.

"What keeps Padre Pio so long?" she asked.

"He is still in church," replied the latter. Then, a bit hesitantly: "But wait, I'll go and see."

As he hurried into the church, the sexton found Padre Pio kneeling behind the altar, his face to the ground and quite oblivious to the world about him. Alarmed, he immediately went in search of the pastor.

"Zi' Tore, the friar is dead!"

"Where?"

"In the church."

"You mind your business and close the door!" said the pastor, who well knew what had happened.

He also knew of the diabolical vexations to which Padre Pio was constantly exposed, especially at night. The two generally spent their evenings together, but around nine o'clock Padre Pio was accustomed to leave for home. Here, when he retired, extraordinary screams and yells were to be heard coming from his room. At first people thought that he was entertaining rowdy friends, and complained to his mother. But she knew the truth. Padre Pio was not entertaining anyone. The fearful disturbance was occasioned by visitors from hell who tormented her poor boy and prevented his praying or sleeping.

As he was entering his room one night, the devil accosted Padre Pio. "Here comes the saint!" he sneered.

"Yes, in spite of you," answered the friar calmly. But he had scarcely spoken the words when he was seized and thrown against the wall, then hurled to the floor and dragged around the room.

At other times the devil would assume human form, as when he appeared as a Capuchin resembling Padre Pio's former confessor. This false friar exhorted Padre Pio to give up his penitential life because God did not approve of it. Surprised at such advice from his spiritual director, Padre Pio had the courage to ask his visitor to say "Blessed be Jesus!" At once the apparition vanished, leaving behind a sulphurous smell.

The friar's real spiritual director, Padre Agostino[2] by name, kept constantly in touch with him during this time, guiding him in the ways of perfection and encouraging him in the struggle against Satan. Another source of courage and comfort was Padre Pio's Guardian Angel, who visibly assisted him and with his heavenly light dispelled the gloom and the darkness caused by the devil's assaults.

Late every afternoon it was customary for Padre Pio to take a walk with Zi' Tore, the pastor, at which time the two would talk about their favorite subjects. On one such occasion the Angelus was ringing. The two priests had just reached the site where many years before there had been a Capuchin monastery. Having said the Angelus, Padre Pio suddenly stopped

---

[2] This Father Agostino became, years later, the Father Guardian of the Monastery of San Giovanni Rotondo, Padre Pio's immediate superior.

and looked towards heaven, as though listening to a mysterious voice.

"Piuccio, what do you see, what do you hear?" asked the pastor.

The young friar smiled thoughtfully. "The sound of these bells reminds me of the bells that once used to ring here. Somehow I feel another monastery will rise on this spot, more beautiful and much larger than the old one."

"And when will this happen, Piuccio?"

"I don't know, Father, but I feel it will happen some day."

This prophecy has now been fulfilled, for on May 21, 1951, the church of the new Capuchin monastery of Pietrelcina was dedicated by Archbishop A. Mancinelli of Benevento.

Political events of very great importance began to disturb everyone's peace of mind during the summer of 1914. The spark that precipitated the first world conflict was ignited with Austria's declaration of war on Serbia, July 28, 1914. Overcome more by these events than by age, Pope Pius X died on August 20 of that year. On May 24, 1915, Italy entered the war against Austria. Padre Pio could not fail to experience the agony of those days even before his personal participation in the struggle. He multiplied his prayers and his penances, asking God to let him suffer and to spare others.

During the long summer days of 1915, Padre Pio used to spend many hours under a tree on the family farm outside Pietrelcina. Here, on September 20, when he had been reading and praying all alone, he suddenly felt stabbing and burning pains in both his hands and feet and on his left side under his heart. His mother was calling him home for dinner when she noticed her son in great agony, shaking both hands as if trying to cool them. There was no mark of any sort, and no blood in those places, and so she did not become alarmed but simply asked: "How do you feel? What's the matter with your hands?"

"I'm all right," was the reply. "I just feel some stabbing pains in my hands."

As he spoke, Padre Pio tried to smile and later ate the meal his mother had prepared without further discussion of what had happened; however, he did confide in his confessor, the Archpriest Zi' Tore. This good old man, when he had heard everything, exclaimed: "Ha, Piuccio, who knows what may happen to you one of these days!"

He had understood the meaning of those five mystical wounds, the invisible stigmata that were a prelude to the real wounds that would appear on Padre Pio's body exactly three years later when he was living in his monastery at San Giovanni Rotondo.

PADRE PIO IN HIS YOUTH

Chapter Five

Military Interlude

THE drafting of young priests for military service went hand in hand with the drafting of other young men during the war years in Italy, with the difference that a priest was assigned almost exclusively to the Medical Corps if he was not given a commission as military chaplain. In the spring of 1916 when this writer, already a priest, had to report for duty in his native military district of Benevento, he saw a number of bearded Capuchins assembled there for the same purpose. One of these was probably Padre Pio himself, for he, too, reported that same year for duty and to the same district.

Because of his poor health, Padre Pio's induction was delayed until December of that year. In a long letter full of advice to some of his spiritual children, dated from Pietrelcina, December 15, 1916, he writes:

"I shall be leaving for Naples tomorrow morning. Accompany me with your continued prayers, and make them always longer, especially during these days of supreme decision."

Then followed a lengthy postscript:

"What can I tell you about myself? I feel such a void in my heart. . . . In the midst of the affectionate care shown me by my family, I notice that the condition is becoming ever more frightful. Oh, My God, I feel the blood freezing in my veins at the mere thought of what may happen to me! I count on your prayers for the good result of my test."[1]

A card written earlier from the military hospital in Naples, (December 12), to the same persons, has this to say:

"I have been visited twice the last few days, and my condition was recognized both times. I am waiting now for a third medical visit, and to tell you the truth, I doubt whether they will defer me this time. God's Will be done! In the meantime, you and all the others double your prayers to our good Lord and the Holy Virgin."[2]

The fears mentioned by Padre Pio were well founded, because he was declared fit for military duty and assigned to the tenth company of the Medical Corps, with headquarters in Naples.

Dressed in a uniform twice his size, he joined the newly enlisted soldiers in the common barracks for the usual general training. After a few days of that life, he took sick and was transferred to the military hospital. Here his high temperature puzzled everyone. Ordinary clinical thermometers always broke when applied to him. Special thermometers had to be used, and they often indicated readings of from 120 to 125 degrees Fahrenheit. Still more baffling was the fact that no delirium or other mental disturbance accompanied such high temperatures.

As soon as Padre Pio was able to travel, he was sent home on a short leave of absence. He presented himself to his Provincial Superior in Foggia, who ordered him to go to Pietrelcina where the air was better and he would be able to have expert care. When his leave of absence expired, he returned to Naples. Here

---

[1] *Ho visto Padre Pio,* by Gian Carlo Pedriali, p. 87.
[2] Ibidem.

he was re-examined and given a new leave of absence for six months. This interval was spent in part with his family in Pietrelcina, in part at the Capuchin monastery in San Giovanni Rotondo.

His papers said to wait for further instruction at the end of his leave. When the six months were over, Padre Pio was still waiting for these instructions. In the meantime, the police had been notified to look for a soldier named Francesco Forgione who had overstayed his leave of absence in Pietrelcina. By now the name of Francesco Forgione had been forgotten by all the townspeople. Everyone, including the police, his great friends, knew him as Padre Pio and nothing else. After a long and useless search, the officers finally informed the authorities that there was no soldier by the name of Francesco Forgione in Pietrelcina.

"There must be," was the answer. "Look again."

So once more the police went through the town asking the futile question. Then one morning they met Padre Pio's married sister Felicia.

"Donna Felicia, do you know a soldier named Francesco Forgione?" they asked.

The woman smiled. "Of course. He is my brother Padre Pio, who is now in San Giovanni Rotondo."

The astonished officers were indeed happy to unload the responsibility of this case on their comrades of that distant town. But here the same confusion and equivocation followed, so that finally Padre Pio was declared a deserter from the army. Then one day, while chatting with a Capuchin in front of the monastery of San Giovanni Rotondo and asking the same question, the police finally got their man. Immediately Padre Pio was told to return to his headquarters in Naples. He left the next morning, and when informed by his commanding officer that he was liable to severe punishment for being a deserter, he calmly displayed the document he had received when sent home for convalescence.

"It says here to await further instructions at the expiration of my leave of absence. I have been waiting all this time. Instructions to come to Naples were received yesterday and so here I am."

Seeing the good faith of the Padre, the officer in charge decided to let matters drop.

A few weeks later, Padre Pio was once more in Naples as a patient in the military hospital. After several tests and examinations, he was declared unfit for millitary service, being afflicted with tuberculosis of the lungs. He was not only discharged from service but also given a small pension. However, Padre Pio felt that he could not rightfully accept such a gift from the Government, since he had done nothing in the way of military service to deserve it. But, when told that this money would not go to him but to his monastery, and to the poor children of the town, he consented and signed his name to the necessary papers.

Zi' Orazio, who had already returned from America, wanted to wear his son's discarded military uniform when he worked in the fields. Padre Pio objected, and insisted that it be sent back to headquarters.

So ended the military interlude in Padre Pio's life. He had been a soldier for less than a year, and most of this time had been spent either in the hospital or at home convalescing.

On December 12, 1917, Padre Pio left Pietrelcina for the last time. He felt the separation from his dear ones and from his native town very keenly.

"Good-bye, Mother, I don't know whether I shall return to this home and to you again or not," he said. "I am now in the keeping of the dear Madonna, the Mother of all mothers!"

The same day he reported to the Provincial Superior in Foggia, who assigned him to the Capuchin Monastery of San Giovanni Rotondo, some twenty-five miles north of Foggia on the slope of Mount Gargano. Here he has remained ever since.

Chapter Six

The Stigmata

SAN Giovanni Rotondo was an obscure town of about ten thousand inhabitants when Padre Pio arrived there in December, 1917. The Monastery of Our Lady of Grace is situated about one mile beyond the town itself, on the slope of Mount Gargano, at an altitude of some 2,400 feet. It has a healthful climate and affords a beautiful view of the surrounding countryside. The church of Our Lady of Grace is attached to the monastery, beyond which is a lovely garden enclosed by a wall. A Latin inscription on the frontispiece of the church states that it was rebuilt in the year of Our Lord 1629.[1]

No better title could be found for a church in which so many graces have been dispensed, especially since the day of Padre Pio's arrival there in 1917. Then that mile of road leading from the town to the monastery was a stony and broken path, ascending through a more or less wild country, and flanked by drab olive trees. Now San Giovanni Rotondo is far larger and more prosperous. That one obscure road winding up to the Capuchins has become a beautiful avenue flanked by modern homes and villas, the homes of Padre Pio's spiritual children, men and women who have come from distant countries to live and to die near the church of Our Lady of Grace. In 1939 imposing marble Stations of the Cross were erected along this avenue, a gift from the good people of Bologna to Padre Pio. But the town's

---

[1] Templum hoc Sanctae Mariae Gratiae dicatum reedificatum fuit anno Domini, 1629. Today a new and much larger church has been added. Father Pio is buried in the crypt. Pilgrims come to his tomb from every corner of the world.

most impressive structure is the *Casa Sollievo della Sofferenza*—
The House for the Relief of Suffering—about which we shall
speak in a later chapter.

Padre Pio was sent to San Giovanni Rotondo in order that
he might recover his health, or else die peacefully. In spite of
his weakness, he scrupulously fulfilled all the duties of the community, was always the first in church and at other exercises. In
addition to the discomfort caused by his infirmity, he continued
to suffer the stabbing and burning pains of the invisible stigmata which he had first experienced on September 20, 1915.

The good Father was passing through these many physical
afflictions with humility and patience, well knowing that they
were part of the mystical purgation of his soul, his dark night.
This appears evident from some of his letters written at the
time, before he was forbidden to send or to receive correspondence.

"My poor soul is about to drown in the waters of bitterness,
and I do not see any hope except in the prayers of other people.
Yes, pray and pray with ever-growing insistence to Divine
Goodness that It may have mercy on me and may not recall the
sins of my youth, which God has already forgotten, to punish
them now. Pray that I may be allowed to weep over my miseries and be permitted to deplore the fact that I was ever
born. . . ."

At various times during this period, speaking of his trials,
he says: "The hand of God is upon me!" To this period of in-
ternal darkness belongs the episode mentioned at the beginning
of this book, of his going in search of Jesus through the cor-
ridors of his monastery. It was in this way that he was being
prepared for what was to take place on September 20, 1918.

On this particular morning Padre Pio was kneeling in the

PADRE PIO WAS PRAYING BEFORE THIS CRUCIFIX WHEN HE
RECEIVED THE STIGMATA.

church choir after Mass, making his thanksgiving as usual at the foot of a large crucifix and passing into the contemplation of the Passion and Death of Our Lord. It was the third anniversary of his invisible stigmata, and about the same hour. While asking Our Lord to give him more of His love and more of His pains, five luminous rays from the five wounds of the Crucified suddenly penetrated his hands, feet and side. The pain and the joy experienced at this moment were too great for him to bear. He swooned and fell to the floor, bleeding profusely from his wounds. Brother Nicola came, saw and understood what had happened. He called the superior and with his assistance carried Padre Pio to his cell and laid him on his bed. He was unable to walk and asked to be left alone.

When the local superior had examined the mysterious phenomena, he immediately got in touch with the Provincial Superior in Foggia and the General Superior in Rome. The Provincial ordered that a photograph be taken of the wounds in Padre Pio's hands. This was done, and the picture dispatched to Rome. The same Provincial also ordered that Padre Pio be thoroughly examined by Luigi Romanelli, M.D., of Barletta. This doctor visited Padre Pio five times during the following two years in order to see whether any change had taken place in his condition.

After giving a detailed description of the stigmata (which he calls "lesions"), Dr. Romanelli concludes his report with these words:

"I have visited Padre Pio five different times in fifteen months, and I have not found a clinical symptom that could authorize me to classify those wounds."

The same doctor also observes:

"Scientifically speaking, wounds heal under the proper treatment, and complications set in if they are neglected. Now, can it be scientifically explained why Padre Pio's wounds—treated without any scientific norm—subjected, even in my presence, to washing in water that was anything but sterile—covered with common woolen gloves, or with handkerchiefs taken from the common open shelves without any disinfection and having been washed with soap of the lowest quality—do not fester, show no complications and do not heal?"[2]

This fact was regarded as extraordinary two years after the appearance of those wounds. What must we say now, over 40 years later, when the same wounds persist with no signs of complication?

In October, 1919, George Festa, M.D., was sent from Rome by the Superior General of the Capuchins to visit Padre Pio at San Giovanni Rotondo and to make a complete report on his condition.

"An anatomic lesion of the tissues, in the palm of the left hand, near the middle of the third metacarpus, almost circular in shape with clean-cut borders having a diameter of little more than two centimeters. This lesion appeared then, as it does now, covered by red-brown scabs."

The doctor describes these scabs in the form of radiating scales produced by the progressive drying of the blood that flows slowly from the wound. These scabs fall out from time to time, revealing the wound in all its details. The Provincial Superior, who had himself examined the wounds immediately after their appearance, before any scabs had been formed, said:

"If I were questioned by superior authority on this point, I would state, under oath (such is the certainty of the impression

---

[2] Dr. G. Festa, *Misteri di Scienza e Luci di Fede,* p. 286, f.

I have received), that looking through the wounds in the palms of his—Padre Pio's— hands, one would have been able to see in all its details a piece of writing or another object placed on the opposite side of his hands."[3]

This means that the friar's stigmata are real transfixions or perforating wounds. The contours are so clear that, even under a magnifying glass, they present no edema, no infiltration, no reddening.[4]

The wounds in the feet show the same characteristics as those in the hands. The doctor noticed that it was very difficult and rather painful for Padre Pio to close his hands. The same difficulty is noticed in his gait because of the wounds in his feet. The wound in his side is about two and three-quarters inches in length and has the shape of an inverted cross, such as a cut by a lance would have caused. It is about one inch below the left *papilla mammaria* and offers the same characteristics as the other wounds.

All who have known Padre Pio have called him a saint. Crowds used to flock to the churches of the various monasteries where he had been previously stationed. One of the reasons for sending him so far away into the solitude of Mount Gargano was to remove him from the uncontrollable admiration of the people. But it is difficult to hide a light. Darkness makes its radiance more evident, and there was much darkness in the world in those days, almost as much as now.

The news that Pietrelcina's native son had received the stigmata spread like wildfire, and soon people by the thousands were flocking to see him, to kiss his hands, to go to confession, to assist at his Mass. They came from neighboring towns, then

---

[3] Dr. G. Festa, o. c., p. 166.
[4] Ibidem.

PICTURE TAKEN BY ORDER OF THE SUPERIORS SOON AFTER THE
STIGMATIZATION, 1918.

from the rest of Italy, of Europe, and from other continents. On more than one occasion the police had to be called in to control the crowds and so allow the poor Capuchins a little rest at night.

Pietrelcina was the first town to hear the news of Padre Pio's stigmata. The Archpriest sent for Padre Pio's parents. The sexton went and called Zi' Giuseppa, the mother.

"The pastor wants you to come to his house!"

"What for?"

"He has a letter he wants you to hear."

With two of her children away from home, Zi' Giuseppa thought that one of them must be sick.

"No," said the sexton, "they are all right," and tears came to his eyes.

"What is the matter then?"

"I am crying for joy! Our Padre Pio is a saint! Come and hear the letter!"

Giuseppa went, and the old Archpriest explained what had happened, adding: "I have known it for three years. Remember that day when he came home shaking his hands in agony? He had received the pain of those very same wounds which have now appeared on his body."

Zi' Orazio was working on the farm. When he returned home that evening, he found his wife in tears.

"What's the matter?" he demanded anxiously.

"Nothing. I'm just crying for joy."

"But why?"

"Because our boy is a saint! He has the wounds of Our Lord Jesus Christ!"

Then they both cried. Worthy parents of such a son!

Chapter Seven

Necrobiosis, Hysteria, Stigmatization

STIGMATA, in a mystical sense, are real lesions of skin and tissues, real wounds such as those described in the preceding chapter by Dr. Romanelli and Dr. Festa. By their shape and localization they correspond to the five wounds of the Crucified Christ.

As a common medical term, the word "stigma" means a mark or a spot *on* the skin. More specifically, the hysterical stigma means a *red* spot, due to extravasation of blood produced by nervous influence.[1] From a comparison of the two concepts— theological and medical stigmata—it appears that a vast difference exists between them. However, since one and the same term is used in both cases, those who do not believe in a supernatural cause, or in the possibility of its intervention, will say that the phenomenon is specifically the same in both cases and the cause—nervous influence—is identical. We are convinced that the stigmata of which we are speaking—the case of Padre Pio and similar ones—are specifically different from the stigmata taken in the common medical sense given above, and that the cause must also be specifically different.

For the thousands of faithful and the many beneficiaries of Padre Pio's blessings, his stigmata create no difficulties. These people know that Padre Pio is a saintly priest. Therefore, his

---

[1] These definitions are taken from Taber's Cyclopedic Medical Dictionary.

wounds have a mystical meaning—the seal of Christ on His servant. Nevertheless, it is a duty for Church authorities, when such phenomena take place, to inquire most diligently into the nature of the phenomenon in order to preclude all possibility of fraud and deception, so that people may not be led to regard as supernatural and miraculous what is actually an ordinary effect of natural causes. This will explain the long and tedious series of examinations to which Padre Pio and other stigmatics have been subjected in the past, and the restrictions placed upon them.

The discomfort and physical pain of the stigmata are trifling when compared with the mental suffering caused by suspicion and condemnation. This mental crucifixion is an integral part of the state of a victim soul, and stigmatics are victim souls. To be understood, their case must be taken as a whole. Without the spiritual and mystical element from within, the external corporal phenomenon of stigmatization will never be explained.

During the summer of 1919, the Superior General of the Capuchins requested Amico Bignami, M.D., Ordinary Professor of Pathology at the University of Rome, to visit Padre Pio and to make a complete report on his condition. Dr. Bignami was an unbeliever. He examined Padre Pio with great diffidence, then applied a specific remedy to heal the wounds, completely confident of a successful result. However, as a necessary precaution, he applied a seal to the dressing covering the wounds. After the required time had elapsed, he removed the seal and the dressing, only to find the wounds completely unaffected by his remedy!

In his long report, the doctor pictures Padre Pio as being a very modest man, with an expression of goodness and *sincerity* that inspires confidence. Then, having described the stigmata, he says that they are a pathological manifestation whose cause must be found in one of three possible hypotheses:

1. They could have been produced artificially and voluntarily.
2. They could be the manifestation of a morbid condition.
3. They could be partly the result of a morbid condition and partly artificial.

He excludes the possibility of the first hypothesis in this case. He admits in part the possibility of the second hypothesis and attributes it to a necrosis of the derm and epidermis—his famous theory of *necrobiosis*. The part he cannot reconcile is the fact of the wounds' localization, the symmetrical position in both hands and feet, and the fact that at the time they had persisted there for nearly a year without modification.

What would he say now, after thirty-five years of the same unchanged state of affairs?

Dr. Bignami admits in part the possibility of the third hypothesis, saying that what had started naturally could have been completed and perfected, perhaps unconsciously, by Padre Pio himself, using a chemical similar to iodine. Then, not satisfied with his own explanation, he concludes the examination with a caustic remark:

"Father, tell me, why did these wounds of yours appear in these particular places and not in other parts of your body?"

"Well," replied Padre Pio, without hesitation, "you are a man of science, Doctor, *you* tell me why these wounds should have appeared in other parts of my body and not where they are!"

Dr. Bignami's report did not seem to satisfy the Capuchin authorities in Rome. Thus, in July, 1919, soon after receiving it, the same Superior General requested George Festa, M.D., an eminent Roman doctor, to go to San Giovanni Rotondo to visit Padre Pio. He was not told about Professor Bignami's visit and report.

Early in October Dr. Festa undertook the task assigned to him, stopping first at Foggia to see the Provincial Superior and to examine all the documents pertaining to Padre Pio. Then, in the company of the Provincial, he drove to San Giovanni Rotondo.

He soon noticed the sweet and humble disposition of the stigmatic, and understood that the new phenomenon was actually a source of mortification and humiliation to him. In fact, the friar showed no pleasure or satisfaction in what had happened, regarding it all as a cross.

Dr. Festa not only examined Padre Pio's wounds, as other doctors before him had done, but also remained long enough in the monastery to obtain a good idea of Padre Pio's life and character. On his return to Rome, having seen Dr. Bignami's report and noticing some difference between the latter's description of the stigmata and his own, he decided to visit Padre Pio a second time, and to invite Dr. Romanelli to come and compare conclusions with him. This was done in July, 1920.

The conclusions of the two medical men were in perfect harmony. Five years later Dr. Festa returned to see Padre Pio and found no modification in the conditions of the five wounds as previously described.

Dr. Festa's final report concludes with these words:

"The five lesions which I have observed in Padre Pio must be regarded as true and real anatomic lesions of the tissues. Their persistence, two years after their first appearance, their strange anatomo-pathological characteristics, the constant oozing of very red and very fragrant blood, their localization, coinciding with the parts of the body in which Our Lord offered Himself to the supreme sacrifice of the Cross, are things which may puzzle only those who from natural facts are unable to rise to a synthesis of religion and faith."

The complete report was presented to the ecclesiastical authorities in Rome, and the Superior General of the Capuchins at that time, Father Joseph Anthony of Persiceto, wrote a letter of thanks to Dr. Festa on November 9, 1920:

"I have read your learned and cogent report which you kindly sent me. In it, our good Padre Pio appears as he really is, and he is ably defended against certain hypotheses which obscure instead of explaining the wonderful phenomena that Divine Providence works in him."[2]

The "certain hypotheses" were not only those presented by Dr. Bignami, but especially those of Father A. Gemelli, O.F.M., M.D., the great authority of the time on experimental psychology. Father Gemelli visited Padre Pio, but no report is available on what he found. According to Dr. Festa, who later had a discussion of the case with the Franciscan scientist, Father Gemelli "never had the opportunity of seeing with his own eyes the wounds that Padre Pio has impressed on his body."[3]

---

[2] G. Festa, o.c., p. 271.

[3] Ibid. p. 189. From a letter written by Dr. Festa to Mr. Frederick Abresh, on June 8, 1929, whose original can be seen in Mr. Abresh's store in San Giovanni Rotondo, we translate the three following paragraphs:

"The stigmata are a phenomenon that remains absolutely unexplainable, if by stigmata is to be understood *a reproduction on the human body of the marks of the crucifixion.*

"The ignorant and those who presume to know everything, while knowing nothing, may continue to say what they like, but they will never have in their favor a single good argument to prove the truth of their assertion.

"In so far as the case of our good Padre (Pio) is concerned, the phenomenon far surpasses the limits of even the most exalted discussions,

In that discussion, Father Gemelli maintained that the wounds of Padre Pio could not be classified among those phenomena whose origin is above the ordinary manifestations of nature. His thought was made clearer in an article he published in the periodical *Vita e Pensiero,* October, 1924, on the occasion of the seventh centenary of the stigmatization of Saint Francis of Assisi. The title of his article is the following: *Le stimmate di San Francesco nel giudizio della scienza,* or "A scientific appraisal of the stigmata of Saint Francis."

A scientific refutation of the principles, the conclusions and the implications of this article is given by Dr. Festa in his book on Padre Pio. The January, 1925, issue of the authoritative *La Civiltà Cattolica* calls Gemelli's article "inexact and imprudent." However, in order to cut short all speculations and to forestall abuses (because many went to Padre Pio as to an oracle and divine herald, abuses Padre Pio himself condemned in the people), the Holy Office issued a warning to all the faithful to abstain from going to see Padre Pio and from writing to him because there was not sufficient evidence that the facts attributed to him were supernatural.[4]

Padre Pio was further forbidden to show his wounds to anyone, including doctors, and we shall see how firmly and heroically he adhered to this injunction.

Father Gemelli's authority was very great at that time, and his theory was this: except for Saint Francis of Assisi and Saint Catherine of Siena, most of the other cases of stigmatization in the Church find a reasonable explanation in the diagnosis of hysteria. We refer the reader to the often cited work of

---

[4] AAS, May 31, 1923.
because of the length of time he has worn them—nearly eleven years—*(today, 1965, over 47 years!)* and because of their peculiar and constant anatomical characteristics."

Dr. Festa for a complete and stringent rebuttal of Gemelli's theory in our case. But, because of the general application that this hysteria theory involves, a word must be said here on what hysteria actually is and actually does in the human body.

Among the things which hysteria (and any other nervous influence) cannot produce are wounds or lesions of tissues— i.e., the stigmata, taken in the theological sense, as explained at the beginning of this chapter.

Babinski, one of the most eminent scholars of neuropathology, affirms that hysteria has *never* produced lesions of the skin. The same thing is affirmed by Dujerine, the successor of Charcot at the Salpetrière. In the vast number of cases of psychopathics and neuropathics observed by him at the Salpetrière, there never was a single case of bleeding wounds like the stigmata.[5] The same conclusion was also reached by Dr. Pierre Janet, who, in his twenty-two years of practice among neuropathics, never had a single case of true stigmatization. *Natural* stigmata have never been observed and never produced by experiments.

The defenders of the hysteria theory have been forced to change their position radically, and even Father Gemelli admits, in his article mentioned above, that "it is no longer possible today to affirm that hysteria can produce by itself organic alterations. . . . The stigmata in hysterical persons are produced artificially by them, even though unconsciously." He calls this phenomenon "psittacism." "The sick person procures himself such lesions (the stigmata) by artificial means which we find difficult to discover and to prove."[6]

---

[5] Dujerine: *Manifestations fonctionelles des psychonevroses,* Paris, 1911.

[6] Gemelli: *Le stimmate di San Francesco nel giudizio della scienza, Vita e Pensiero,* October 1924. The theory of "hysterical wounds" produced "by the power of imagination" is rejected by scientists today. Hilda Graef and M. Waldmann still defend it. *The Case of Therese Neumann,* p. xvii and passim.

We should like to ask only one question here: Can a person produce a wound artificially and keep it open and bleeding for more than forty years, without causing any complication and modification in the wound itself, and without ever being discovered? One need not be an expert in order to find the proper answer.[7]

Science, divorced from faith, has often run into the blind alleys of human error, forgetting that there is a limit to all natural forces beyond which we find the hand of the Creator. No matter how strong and violent the blood pressure may be, it will always be arrested in normal conditions by the minute blood vessels at the periphery of the body. The capillary system is the natural boundary to the circulation of the blood established by the Creator. The latest experiments, such as those made by Bouchard, prove that in normal conditions the capillary system can resist all pressure of the blood without injury, and without losing one single drop of blood. The Creator, Who had special care of man and animal life in general, must have made at least the same provision for safety which He made for the ocean waters when He said: "I set my bounds around it, and made it bars and doors: And I said: Hitherto thou shalt come, and shall go no further, and here thou shalt break thy swelling waves."[8]

Hysterical emotions and the "swelling waves" of the heart can never go so far, in normal conditions, as to cause a break in the skin, the natural and ultimate barrier of the body.

According to Dr. Bignami's testimony, one finds in Padre Pio's face an expression of goodness and sincerity that inspires utter confidence. The hysterical person is insincere; simula-

---

[7] We are happy to report that, in later years, Father Gemelli admitted that he was mistaken in regard to the wounds of Padre Pio.

[8] Job, 38:10.

tion and lying are the characteristics of hysteria, certainly not an apt ground for Christian virtue or for sanctity. The virtue of Padre Pio, no less than his goodness and sincerity, is realized by all who have met him. These persons are in the thousands, with many of them eminent in the world of science, literature, art and the hierarchy of the Church.

Very instructive for our case and similar ones is what we read in the life of Saint Gemma Galgani, a stigmatic who died in 1903 and who was canonized in 1940. Doubts and suspicions were entertained by many regarding the nature of her stigmata. Even her own confessor, Bishop Volpi, appealed to science for a decision. This is what Our Lord told Saint Gemma on this occasion:

"Tell the confessor that in the presence of the doctor I will do nothing at all that he wishes."

Despite Gemma's admonition, the doctor was brought in and he pronounced her a victim of hysteria, for when he applied water to the wounds they entirely disappeared. After this visit Gemma wrote to her confessor:

"Jesus spoke to me thus: 'Do you not remember, My daughter, that I told you there would come a day when no one would believe in you any more? Well, this is that day. Oh, how much more acceptable you are to Me thus despised than before when all believed you to be a saint!' "[9]

These mystical elements escape every sort of scientific investigation. The Lord never performs miracles to satisfy human curiosity, even scientific curiosity. Christ before Herod met all the curious questions of that ruler with absolute silence, and did not satisfy his desire to see the performance of a miracle (Luke, 23:8 ff.).

[9] Portrait of Saint Gemma—a Stigmatic, by Sister St. Michael, p. 57 f.

Chapter Eight

The Voice of Obedience

PADRE PIO never said a word in defense of his own case of stigmatization. He left everything to God. Together with his five wounds, a number of other extraordinary phenomena became manifest. It was like a sudden Pentecostal revelation. Those various gifts were like many fiery tongues, like many loud voices proclaiming the power of God. We shall examine these voices, the first of which will be the voice of obedience— a safe guarantee for us that the other voices are not the voices of the deceiver but those of the Master.

In one of his spiritual exhortations, Padre Pio had this to say about the virtue of obedience:

"Where there is no obedience, there is no virtue; where there is no virtue, there is no good; where there is no good, there is no love; where there is no love, there is no God; and where there is no God, there is no Paradise."

Guided by such wisdom, it was not difficult for him to be resigned to the Will of God as manifested in the command received from his ecclesiastical superiors. With obedience he had God and retained the living hope of never-ending bliss; what did he care if everything else was taken from him?

The following episode, witnessed and narrated by the late Dr. G. Festa, gives some idea of the actual heroism of Padre Pio's obedience.

It was towards the end of September, 1925. At this time

Padre Pio was under obedience to keep his five wounds covered and not to permit any doctor to examine them. At this same time Dr. Festa, having been sick himself for quite a while, decided to go to San Giovanni Rotondo to rest both body and soul in the company of Padre Pio. It was a friendly social call, not a professional one, during which the medical man stayed at the monastery in a little cell only four doors beyond that of Padre Pio. It was a rather poor place for a famous Roman doctor to spend his convalescence, but the presence of the good Padre and the rest of the Capuchin community was sufficient recompense for whatever else was lacking.

On October 1, Dr. Festa was having a conversation with Padre Pio, interspersing it with humorous and witty remarks (Padre Pio has a great sense of humor), when suddenly the friar became very serious.

"I have been sick and suffering atrocious pains for a very long time," he declared. "Please, do me the favor of examining me."

Dr. Festa complied with the request and found that his good friend had a voluminous and irreducible hernia, with extensive adhesions, as well as peritonitis in the right inguinal region. He immediately suggested a surgical operation.

"It's too bad that I didn't tell you about all this earlier," said Padre Pio, "because I did intend to ask you to do me this favor."

Accepting his request, Dr. Festa spoke to the Guardian that night and it was decided to have the operation performed as soon as possible. But it would have to take place in the monastery, since Padre Pio was not allowed to leave his conventual home. Accordingly, the doctor dispatched a friend to Rome to get everything necessary for the operation, which would take place on October 5.

In the intervening days, Dr. Festa begged Padre Pio to ask Our Lord if it was all right for him to perform the delicate operation, or whether a better doctor was needed. Padre Pio replied that he would never ask Our Lord such a thing.

"He has already spoken in this respect, when He said that we should love one another. Is it not charity on your side to do for me what you have promised to do? Carry out your plans, and the Lord will not fail to bless your hand."

So, preparations were completed, and a local doctor, Angelo Merla (formerly an atheist and Freemason, now a convert of Padre Pio), was asked to assist Dr. Festa. A freshly painted room in the monastery was also made ready for the operation.

On October 5, Padre Pio followed the customary routine of all his other days. He rose at 3:30 in the morning for his prayers and preparation for Mass. He sang High Mass at six, heard a large number of confessions until noon, then finally walked up to the improvised operating room where the medical men and aides were waiting.

"Well, now I'm at your disposal," he told them cheerfully. "But, please, no chloroform."

No one could convince him to change his mind on this point, and he assured the two physicians that he would remain motionless during the operation, no matter in what position they put him.

The reason for such an attitude soon became manifest when the patient asked one question of Dr. Festa:

"Tell me, will you refrain from examining my wounds—the stigmata—once you have me under the influence of chloroform?" (At this time he had been forbidden to show them to any doctor.)

Five years had passed since Dr. Festa had examined the wounds, and now he readily admitted his great curiosity to see them again. Yes, he had planned on a thorough scrutiny before the operation.

"Ah, you see, now, how right I was in refusing an anesthetic," said Padre Pio amiably.

The above mentioned prohibition to show his wounds had been issued by the Holy Office for reasons of prudence, and in order to control the immoderate behavior of the crowds that visited San Giovanni Rotondo. Unfortunately, many people regarded this prohibition as reflecting on the virtue of the Padre and the nature of his wounds. Nevertheless, despite their malicious gossip, Padre Pio continued to obey the command from Rome. Generally speaking, this was not too difficult, but on October 5, 1925, his obedience entailed nearly two hours of martyrdom. Yet he suffered that martyrdom rather than offer the occasion for an order of the Sacred Congregation to be disregarded. This was the price of his obedience, and he paid it without a word of complaint during the long ordeal. Only at the cutting of the hernial sac, and of the adhesions, two big tears ran down his cheeks.

"Jesus, forgive me if I do not know how to suffer as I should!" he was heard to say.

When the operation was over, Padre Pio collapsed and became unconscious. The operation was successful and the recovery both speedy and complete. Six days later he was declared cured, and after a brief period of convalescence he resumed his daily routine.

When the Padre refused anesthesia, Dr. Festa offered him a

small glass of Benedictine cordial, and when the doctor insisted that he should take a little more, Padre Pio answered: "No more. I'm afraid that the Benedictine may not agree with the Capuchin!"

Dr. Festa confesses, as he had candidly admitted to Padre Pio, that he could not resist his professional curiosity to re-examine the stigmata, which had been the object of his study five years before, and so he took advantage of Padre Pio's swooning after the operation to take a look at the five wounds. He found the identical characteristics as on his previous examinations, except that one difference was observed in the wound on the left side under the heart. Here the scabs had fallen and the wound appeared clear and fresh, with evident signs of a *luminous radiation* all along the borders—a phenomenon previously reported by Dr. L. Romanelli.

Merciful nature afforded the opportunity which Padre Pio had absolutely denied at the cost of immense suffering to himself in order to obey the Church. This, the voice of his obedience!

Chapter Nine
The Voice of the Blood

MANIFOLD and eloquent is the voice of the blood, if we may speak of voice where no sound is uttered. The blood that has been oozing from Padre Pio's wounds all these years, silently and constantly, has its own particular voice—a fragrance of lilies and roses, a sweet odor so pungent and so pleasing that even children have noticed it, and children do not easily become the victims of auto-suggestion. (Neither do professional men, such as the many doctors who have examined Padre Pio).

We quote from the official report made by one of these, Dr. Luigi Romanelli:

"As I was introduced for the first time to Padre Pio in the month of June, 1919, I noticed a certain fragrance coming from his body, so that I said to the Very Reverend Father E. E. of Valenzano (who was with me) that it didn't seem right for a friar, especially one held to possess great sanctity, to make use of perfumes."[1]

After this observation, Dr. Romanelli did not experience any sweet smell for the next two days, even when he was in Padre Pio's cell and seated very close to him. Before leaving, however, a wave of the same sweet fragrance surrounded him for a few minutes as he was going upstairs. Nobody had told him of the existence of this phenomenon, so there could be no auto-suggestion. Had there been such a thing, he would have per-

---

[1] Dr. G. Festa, o.c., p. 282.

ceived that perfume every time he was near Padre Pio, which was not the case.

Dr. Festa is another dependable witness who confirms whatever has been reported by hundreds of people concerning this phenomenon. Being himself completely deprived of the sense of smell, he made no mention of it in his first report, in which he states only the facts which had come to his personal attention. He does say, however, that Padre Pio has never made use of perfume or scented soap at any time. He also reports that after his first visit to Padre Pio, he took away a piece of linen saturated with blood from the Padre's side wound for microscopic study at his office in Rome. The piece of cloth was enclosed in a tube and carried in his brief case. In the public conveyance in which he was riding on leaving San Giovanni Rotondo, there were several other persons, including an army officer, who knew nothing of what he was carrying. In spite of the strong ventilation in the running vehicle, everyone immediately remarked that the characteristic perfume of Padre Pio's blood was in the air.

In the doctor's office in Rome, where the piece of cloth was kept, the air soon became so saturated with the sweet odor that many became curious, and inquired as to its source. A lady who wanted to consult the doctor, not knowing his address, looked it up in the telephone directory of Rome, where two physicians of the same name were listed. Not knowing which of these was connected with Padre Pio's case, she decided to drive to both places. By chance she went first to the real Dr. G. Festa's home. As the door was opened by the maid, she immediately perceived Padre Pio's familiar perfume. At once she realized she had chosen the correct address.

The natural smell of human blood is anything but pleasant,

even when still fresh. But when decomposition sets in, the odor becomes positively offensive. We do not believe that the perfume-like quality of Padre Pio's blood can be naturally explained, especially in view of the striking details which follow.

It has been attested by many witnesses worthy of belief that this characteristic perfume has often been perceived hundreds of miles away from San Giovanni Rotondo, where Padre Pio now spends all his time. This perfume has the function of a voice, as it were—a voice which tells that Padre Pio is thinking of some particular person, i.e., that he is praying for and taking an interest in the problems of that person. It is like his aura, which indicates that he is more than morally present, even though physically very far away.

We shall mention one instance of this phenomenon as narrated by Alberto Del Fante, the great biographer of Padre Pio, who is also his convert and very devoted disciple.

It was the night of February 28, 1931, when Del Fante and his family had returned home from a visit to his parents who, like himself, lived in Bologna. Since it was a Saturday night, Del Fante thought that he would work longer than usual and then rest in the morning by going to a late Mass. Having decided to write until 3:00 a.m., he sat down at his desk and automatically set to work, his wife and children now having retired to their rooms.

Presently he was aware that a sweet perfume was filling the air. At once he recognized the "voice" of Padre Pio who had made him promise never to start any work without first blessing himself. (On this occasion Del Fante had forgotten to do so.)

Without explaining what had happened, he called his family and the maid into his office and asked them whether they noticed anything unusual in the room. Immediately his wife, his older daughter and the maid replied that they smelled a very sweet and perfume-like incense. However, his younger daughter Flora perceived nothing.

In Christian hagiography, this phenomenon is not new. It is the odor of sanctity, taken in the physical sense of the word. Since this odor is directly connected with Padre Pio's stigmata and the blood flowing from them, not from the blood of other accidental wounds, it can well be regarded as "a voice from heaven" attesting to the supernatural origin of the stigmata. It is perceived not only by those who believe in Padre Pio, but also by those who are unwilling or unable to believe.

For instance, Gian Carlo Pedriali, in his little book *Ho Visto Padre Pio* (I Have Seen Padre Pio), tells us that he went to San Giovanni Rotondo merely out of curiosity, and in a rather spiteful frame of mind. He was in church when he first saw Padre Pio coming in the door and being greeted by a crowd of people. He himself was standing at some distance away with his little boy.

"A sharp, yet pleasant odor of blood invaded my nostrils," he writes, "and my little boy, pulling my sleeve asked: 'Papa, what is this perfume?' "[2]

Nobody can suspect either the father or the child of auto-suggestion. The first did not believe at the time—he did later —the other was still unable to believe.

Another visitor of the good Padre was trying to summarize the impressions of his visit several months after his return home. One thing in particular stood out in his mind: the memory of Padre Pio offering Mass, with "that drop of red blood from the wound on the back of his hand trickling down." Here again, the voice of the blood!

---

[2] o.c., p. 40.

In 1928, Zi' Giuseppa—Padre Pio's affectionate mother— was nearly seventy years old, but still in perfect health. She had always wished to die in the arms of her saintly son, but the existing command that forbade him to leave his monastery seemed to make this an impossible hope. However, on Christmas Eve of that same year, she decided to visit her son and to assist at the Midnight Mass which he would celebrate in the church of Our Lady of Grace.

Great joy filled the heart of the good old mother on once more seeing her boy at the altar, this time bearing in his body the "Wounds of Our Lord Jesus Christ." But it was to be the last such joy. Coming out of the church that night, exposed to the cold wind from the mountains, she contracted pneumonia. The best of medical care was to no avail, and she died at San Giovanni Rotondo on January 3, 1929, in a house not far from the Monastery of Our Lady of Grace, assisted to the end by Padre Pio as she had always desired.

Note: Padre Pio wept when his mother died even though he was given to know that her soul was in Heaven. Amazed at the degree of his sorrow friends wondered what to say. Padre Pio himself gave them to understand sympathy for all who suffer the present partings of this life even though they will be followed by the joys of eternal reunion.

Chapter Ten

The Voice of His Converts

THE words of Pope Benedict XV, spoken at a private audience given in 1921 to Monsignor Fernando Damiani, the Vicar General of the diocese of Salto, Uruguay, had a prophetic meaning in view of the extraordinary number of conversions effected by the grace of God through the instrumentality of Padre Pio. These are the words, translated from the Spanish, which were spoken by the Holy Father on the occasion in question:

"Padre Pio is truly an extraordinary man, one of those men God sends from time to time into this world to convert people."

Benedict XV was not only a very able diplomat, but also an excellent judge and appraiser of persons and situations. He pronounced his firm opinion on Padre Pio at a time when many critics, even some ecclesiastics, were busily looking for natural explanations of the various phenomena. Looking back now, three decades later, we realize the importance of those words in the light of events which have taken place since then at San Giovanni Rotondo.

Alberto Del Fante, in his two volumes on Padre Pio: *Per La Storia* (*For the History*), and *Fatti Nuovi* (*New Facts*), tells of at least one hundred extraordinary cures attributed to Padre Pio, giving detailed descriptions of the cases, authentic letters from the persons involved and often the medical certificate confirming the cure. At least some of these accounts are historically well documented, and give a sufficient assurance of truth, but they remain only a human document of human interpretation of facts. Only the Church can tell us what is miraculous and extraordinary in a cure and what is not, because a miracle always implies direct divine intervention, and only the Church can assure us of this circumstance. We shall abstain, therefore, from reporting any such miraculous cures, except where they indirectly concern a conversion.

When atheists, bitter enemies of the Church and habitual sinners change their conduct at a word or at a look from Padre Pio, sometimes even at the mere mention of his name and his virtue, we have something as extraordinary as a miracle—a moral miracle of grace which everybody can see and understand. It is of such miracles that we intend to write now, giving not all, but only a few of the most outstanding conversions made by the holy Capuchin.

Alberto Del Fante, whose name and books we have already mentioned, was an atheist and a Freemason, a lawyer and a journalist by profession. At a time when many Italian papers were reporting extraordinary facts about Padre Pio, he, without knowing the Padre, began to write articles against him. Thus, in his own words:

"Several years ago, without even knowing the Father—Padre Pio—I wrote some articles against him in the Florentine paper *Italia Laica*. At that time I thought him to be an impostor, a cunning man knowing how to deceive simple folk who are too easily moved to enthusiasm. Then there occurred the *unexpected, unmistakable* and *indisputable* healing of my nephew which made me think. . . . The undeniable truth is that my nephew, from being dangerously ill, has now become a frisky, healthy, happy boy."[1]

---

[1] *From Doubt to Faith*, by A. Del Fante, p. 7.

Del Fante then went to San Giovanni Rotondo to see the famous friar with his own eyes—still very skeptical, still an atheist. Being a baptized Catholic, however, he began to feel the call of grace. More to please his relatives than for his own good, he decided to go to confession to Padre Pio.

"Father . . . though I never had a religious faith, I have, nevertheless, always acted honestly."

"Honestly? Even when you. . . ?"

And here Padre Pio reminded his penitent of many things he could not have possibly known, save through divine enlightenment.

The following morning Del Fante went to Mass and received Holy Communion.

"At the moment I was going to receive Holy Communion, being in a corner somewhat removed from the Father, who had to stretch out his arm so that his hand became entirely visible, I could perceive the wound out of which the blessed fragrant blood flows. Something like an electric current went through my body, and my conscience was flooded with waves of joy and sweetness. I felt happier than I had ever been in all my life, as happy as I am now while writing of him. . . . I can truly say that this Communion was the most devout of my life after the first one of my boyhood."[2]

The above incident took place on November 2, 1930. It was the first time that Del Fante had gone from Bologna, his home town, to San Giovanni Rotondo to see Padre Pio. He not only came back to the Faith and to the Sacraments of the Church but he also became a disciple of Padre Pio, and his ardent defender.

---

[2] o.c., p. 16.

His first book on the holy friar was published without an *Imprimatur*. This was due to the fact that, as a lay person, Del Fante did not know of canon 1399, 5, of the Code of Canon Law which requires a previous approval by ecclesiastical authority of all books dealing with miracles, mystical phenomena, revelations, etc. Because of this, the book was forbidden, like several others of the same type. This naturally contributed to the false opinion that the prohibition of these books reflected on the virtue of Padre Pio himself, whereas it was due to the failure of the writers to comply with the requirements of Canon Law. We are told that *Per La Storia,* in the later editions made by Del Fante, has been cleared from censure.[3]

In a letter received by this writer in the month of November, 1951, Del Fante wrote: "Returning this morning from San Giovanni Rotondo, my *thirtieth* trip there to see the Very Reverend Padre Pio di Pietrelcina, I find more than one hundred letters on my desk. . . ."

It was not an ephemeral change, a short-lived conversion, but a permanent and ever-growing attachment to faith and good living.

---

[3] The answer given by the Sunday issue of *Osservatore Romano,* February 22, 1948, telling that there is no longer any prohibition against visiting Padre Pio or writing to him, adds the following remark: "The two books by Del Fante and the one by Festa (on Padre Pio) have the value of a purely human and subjective documentation, and this is the reason why they do not carry the Imprimatur of ecclesiastical authority." This remark seems to exempt the books in question from the requirements of canon 1399, 5, because of their specific nature and form. The two books by Del Fante are *Per la Storia* and *Fatti Nuovi.* The one by Dr. Festa is *Misteri di scienza e luci di Fede.* Del Fante's first publication on Padre Pio: *A Padre Pio di Pietrelcina, l'Araldo del Signore,* was forbidden (AAS, 23, 233, May 1931). For the same reason, these earlier books were also forbidden: *Padre Pio da Pietrelcina,* by G. De Rossi (AAS, 18, 196, April 23, 1926), and *Padre Pio da Pietrelcina,* by Giuseppe Cavaciocchi (Ibid., 308).

A well-known attorney of Genoa, Comm. Cesare Festa, a first cousin of Dr. G. Festa of Rome, former mayor of Arenzano and one of the most prominent Freemasons of Genoa, was one of the first conquests of Padre Pio's kindness and zeal. Dr. G. Festa had often exhorted his cousin to abandon Freemasonry and to return to the Church, but to no avail. When he became acquainted with Padre Pio, he spoke about the Padre to his cousin Cesare. One day, out of curiosity, Cesare left Genoa and traveled all the way south to San Giovanni Rotondo.

"What, *you* here? You, who are a Freemason?" exclaimed Padre Pio the moment he laid eyes on the newcomer.

"Yes, Father," said Cesare.

"And what is your intention as a Freemason?"

"To fight against the Church from a political point of view."

Padre Pio smiled, took his visitor's hand and with extreme kindness began to tell him the story of the Prodigal Son. That same day Cesare went down on his knees before Padre Pio and made his confession, the first in twenty-five years. The next morning he received Holy Communion.

For a few days he remained with the Padre to strengthen his soul for the ordeal that lay ahead. Padre Pio advised him to wait before announcing his official break with the Freemasons. After a few months he returned again to see the Padre, and this time he stopped in Rome to tell his cousin, Dr. Festa, of his conversion and change of heart.

When an Italian pilgrimage to Lourdes was organized under the leadership of Archbishop Achille Ratti of Milan (later Pope Pius XI), Cesare decided to offer his services to the invalid pilgrims, both on the train and later at the hotel. This fact soon became known, and the Socialist paper *Avanti* and similar sheets let loose a violent attack under a big headline: "A Freemason at Lourdes!"

Cesare was immediately requested to explain his actions. His answer was brief and to the point. At Lourdes, he said, he had admired not so much the restoration of bodily health as the miracles of faith. A new storm followed, because, officially, he was still a member of the brotherhood. As he was preparing to go to the last meeting of the Lodge to break all ties with Freemasonry, he received a most encouraging letter from Padre Pio.

"Never be ashamed of Christ or of His doctrine. It is time to fight with open face. May the Giver of all blessings grant you the needed strength!"

These words, coming at such a critical moment, gave Cesare the necessary courage. He went to the Lodge and there, with great fervor of spirit, spoke openly of Christ, the Saviour of the world, of His doctrine, His Church, and of his own supreme happiness in returning to them. Then he officially presented his resignation from office and broke all ties with the sect.

All this took place during November, 1921. The following Christmas Cesare was in Rome with his cousin, Dr. Festa. There the former Freemason was to be seen in the garb of a Franciscan Tertiary, walking in the procession of the Bambino in the church of Ara Coeli, a lighted candle in his hand. Three days later he was received in an audience by Pope Benedict XV, to whom he described his conversion through the good offices of Padre Pio.

"Yes," said the Pope, "Padre Pio is truly a man of God; some have doubts about him, but you will help to make him better known."

Only half a block away from the Capuchin monastery in San

Giovanni Rotondo is a book shop, owned by a distinguished photographer, Signor Federico Abresch. A German by birth and a former Protestant, he has long been a convert to the Catholic Faith. However, his conversion made at the time of his marriage to a Catholic girl had really been rather a formality than a sincere change of mind on his part.

In 1928 Signor Abresch came from Bologna, where he had a photographic studio, to visit Padre Pio. Kneeling down for confession, he simply expressed his unbelief, saying that he regarded confession as a good social institution and no more, not a divine means of grace.

Padre Pio looked at him with an expression of extreme pain. "Heresy! All your Communions have been sacrilegious!" he exclaimed. "You need a general confession. Examine your conscience. Jesus was more merciful to you than to Judas." And with these words he dismissed him.

The poor man felt terribly confused, for he was unable to remember the last time he had made a good confession since entering the Church. When he returned to Padre Pio again, he explained his plight as best he could. Then, very kindly, Padre Pio told him what he could not remember. He had made his last good confession when he had returned from his wedding trip, something which the friar could never have known through natural means.

It was exactly so, as Signor Abresch now remembered the circumstances of that confession. From this point on, Padre Pio began to enumerate the other sins of commission and omission of the penitent before him, concluding with these words: "You have glorified Satan, and Jesus in His boundless love broke His neck for you!"

Signor Abresch then received his penance and absolution,

and with them such a joy and happiness that he felt like a new person. From then on he went to daily Mass and Communion, and finally became a Franciscan Tertiary.

"I believe now," he writes, "not only all the dogmas of the Catholic Church but even her smallest ceremonies. And I feel that if anybody should attempt to take this Faith from me, he could only take my life!"[4]

Signor Abresch and his family, like so many other converts of Padre Pio, wished one thing more—to be able to live near the Padre. Those who cannot afford a move to San Giovanni Rotondo are satisfied with frequent visits there; those who can, settle down in the shadow of the Monastery of Our Lady of Grace—which explains the presence of Signor Abresch in San Giovanni Rotondo today. Most of the photographs published in this book are his property, and he has kindly permitted us to use them. He must exercise great skill to secure these photos, especially those taken during Mass, because Padre Pio never poses and will never knowingly allow anyone to take his picture.

Dr. Angelo M. Merla was one of the doctors who assisted Dr. Festa in the operation performed on Padre Pio which we have already described. He had been an unbeliever, and for thirty years had stayed away from the Church. Padre Pio brought him back to the Sacraments and to regular religious practices. He made his First Communion at the same time as his little daughter. Today, in his office, Dr. Merla often shows people a thermometer which broke when he tried to take the extraordinary temperatures of Padre Pio. (These, at times, reach 120 degrees Fahrenheit.)

Concerning other conversions brought about by Padre Pio, Dr. G. Festa relates that he saw, with his own eyes, how a

---

[4] A. Del Fante, o.c., p. 309 ff.

young Jew knelt before Padre Pio one day and said: "Padre, I won't leave here until you baptize me!" He had come to San Giovanni Rotondo out of curiosity; he went home a Christian.

Another famous conversion is that of Dino Segre, a popular Italian playwright whose pen name is Pitigrilli. After his return to the Faith, he canceled five of his works which had been inspired by gross materialism. He explains the reason for this in his latest book: *Pitigrilli parla di Pitigrilli—Pitigrilli talks about Pitigrilli.*

On page 176 of this book we read:

"I could mention other cases (of conversions made by Padre Pio) and other names that would take us too far, and I would never finish, because every day something new happens there that completely overturns whatever science teaches us. Atheists are suddenly converted, bad people are placed on the right path again. . . ."

On page 173 he tells how he first heard of Padre Pio. It was on the occasion of a visit to Luigi Antonelli, another Italian writer, who lived in Foggia. Antonelli told him how the doctors had found a cancer on the side of his neck. Distressed beyond words, he had asked about his chances for recovery.

"Tell me the truth, how long can I expect to live?"

"Six months with an operation, three months without one."

As preparations for the operation were being made, someone suggested that he go to see Padre Pio and ask his prayers. After all, Foggia was only twenty-five miles distant from San Giovanni Rotondo. Desperate, Antonelli went to the little town, assisted at the Padre's Mass, then made his confession.

"What he—Padre Pio—told me then is hard to express, because at the time I felt as though I were living in another world. The cancer was cured."

Hearing this story, Pitigrilli himself went to see Padre Pio and assisted at his Mass.

"The Mass said by Padre Pio brings tears to the eyes of everyone present," he writes.

Hidden away among the faithful, completely unknown to all, including Padre Pio, Pitigrilli followed the sacred ceremonies. Then at the end of the Mass, Padre Pio suddenly turned around and addressed the congregation in a firm tone of voice.

"Pray, brethren, pray fervently for someone who is here among you today who is in great need of prayer," he said. "One day he will approach the Eucharistic Table and will bring many with him who have been in error like himself."

The people prayed, Padre Pio did the rest, and Pitigrilli returned to the practices of the Catholic Church. Completely reformed as a man and as a writer, he went back to Buenos Aires where he had been living for many years.

On October 27, 1950, there was a funeral in the Church of Our Lady of Grace adjoining the monastery of the Capuchins in San Giovanni Rotondo. The deceased was a young woman, Italia Betti, Ordinary Professor of Mathematics at the Galvani High School of Bologna, and until recently an ardent apostle of Marx and Lenin. A fanatic Communist, always first on the scene on her motorcycle whenever there was a clash in the streets of Bologna between the Communists and the Catholic party, Italia was ready at all times to fight and, if necessary, even to kill. Then she became very sick and the doctors held out no hopes for a recovery. Her younger sister Emerita, also a teacher, was the only one in the Betti family who had remained loyal to the Catholic Faith. This young woman told her sister about Padre Pio and finally prevailed upon her to pay him a visit.

On December 14, 1949, Italia set out from Bologna, accompanied by her mother and sister, to meet Padre Pio. (He had recently appeared to her in a dream!) The three put up in a little house near the monastery. Padre Pio visited, comforted and instructed the former apostle of Communism. He brought light and peace into the heart that had never known them. From his hands she received the Sacraments, then made a public abjuration of her former ways of hatred and error. She was completely resigned to God's Will, and during the remaining ten months of her life gave a wonderful example of humility and patience in her painful sickness. She never left San Giovanni Rotondo. Before she died, she asked to be received into the Third Order of Saint Francis.

Purged in the Blood of the Lamb and in the long painful suffering of her illness, the former Communist passed from this life on October 26, 1950. After the funeral in the church of the Capuchin monastery, she was buried in the cemetery of San Giovanni Rotondo, not far from the grave of Padre Pio's mother.

Italia Betti was known throughout all Italy, and in other parts of Europe, too. She was completely abandoned by the Communists the day she first went to Padre Pio, but Italian Catholics gave her such manifestations of solidarity and affection after her return to the Church as she had never known among those who have lost both the Faith and the love of Christ.

Note: The following pages speak of Father Pio's daily life as witnessed at the time. The editors decided not to re-write these pages after Father Pio's death. We trust that the reader will find the reality of Father Pio in being transported back to the "present" of his daily life.

Chapter Eleven

The Voice of Duty, The Mass, The Confessions

THE life of Padre Pio, since his arrival at the Monastery of Our Lady of Grace in December, 1917, to the present day, has been simple, austere, uniform. He takes part in all the community exercises except the long office in choir after dinner: i.e., Vespers, Compline, Matins and Lauds. (It is too hard for him to stand so long because of the wounds in his feet.)

According to his superior, Padre Pio is always one of the first at the community exercises. He is often already in choir when the other friars arrive, and he remains there in prayer when they retire. After the community's very frugal evening meal (at which he takes less than anyone else) and a brief recreation with his fellow-religious, he retires first to the church for prayer and meditation, and then to his Cell where he reads, prays and attends to other duties until a very late hour of the night.

He does not sleep more than three or four hours, and generally rises at 3:30 a.m. At this time he says the Little Hours and prepares for Mass in his cell. Then he goes to the sacristy at about five o'clock to vest for Mass. He rarely says Mass at the High Altar, but chooses instead one of the small side altars, generally the altar of Saint Francis. Exteriorly his Mass is the same as that of any other priest, but there are a few circumstances and certain qualities in the manner in which he offers the Holy Sacrifice that distinguish it and make it unique.

The duration of his Low Mass is from one hour and fifteen minutes to one hour and thirty minutes . Except for a very long Memento of the Living, the first half of the Mass up to the Consecration is characterized only by extreme attention and devotion. But from the time of the Consecration on, the mystical drama of Calvary is reenacted in an exceptionally vivid and touching manner. It is then that Padre Pio is revealed to the world as the great victim soul, the first stigmatized priest in history, the spiritual phenomenon of our twentieth century.

During Mass (and then only) Padre Pio takes off the half gloves that he wears to cover the wounds in his hands. These wounds, together with those in his feet and in his side, now become especially painful. Agony is written in his face, and many are moved to tears at the sight of the fresh blood flowing from his hands when he raises the Sacred Host and the chalice at the elevation.

Padre Pio's suffering and crucifixion are renewed daily with the renewal of Christ's death. From the time of the elevation begin those long pauses of ecstatic contemplation, of tears, prayers and supplications. This is the high point of the day in San Giovanni Rotondo, the time of immense grace and extraordinary conversions, the time when the blood speaks louder than the most eloquent sermon. Unbelievers watching Padre Pio at the altar have learned that the Mass is a work of consuming love, the love of God for man, and they have believed.

Every morning the little church of the Capuchins is crowded with people, many being converts of Padre Pio who have come from far-away lands to make their home near him. Dearer than all the gold in the world is this privilege to assist at his Mass, to receive the Eucharistic Lord from his hands and to ʾe blessed by those same hands.

THANKSGIVING AFTER HIS MORNING MASS.

People close in about the altar when the Padre says Mass in order to watch everything he does with rapt attention. Only Petruccio, the young blind man who is often to be seen walking with Padre Pio, stays far back in a dark corner of the church.

"Petruccio, wouldn't you like to be able to see again?" Padre Pio once asked his young friend.

"I want my sight only if it is good for my soul," replied Petruccio.

The boy's sight has never come back, but he smiles and is satisfied with the inner light which he has found since his vision left him.

After Mass, Padre Pio returns to the sacristy. Everybody follows to receive his blessing and to kiss his hands before he covers them again with the half gloves. A half hour is spent in thanksgiving after Mass, but often ecstasy sets in and the half hour stretches on and on. It was during such an ecstatic period that Padre Pio received the stigmata in September, 1918.

When his thanksgiving is completed (he takes nothing for breakfast save an occasional glass of water), Padre Pio begins to hear confessions. In all these years, when not forced to lie in bed because of sickness, Padre Pio has heard confessions morning and afternoon. Indeed, most of his priestly life has been spent in the confessional or at the altar. Ordinarily he first hears the confessions of men in the sacristy without a confessional, as is customary in Italy, then he hears the women in the confessional until about noon.

Experience has taught the Capuchins to use various means in order to handle the impatient and enthusiastic crowds of penitents waiting to be heard by the Padre. Recently an iron rail was built around the women's confessional. All who

CROWDS WAITING THEIR TURN TO GO TO CONFESSION

plan to go to confession, both men and women, must register the day beforehand at the monastery office and procure numbered tickets. Leaflets containing practical rules and advice are also distributed, one pertinent admonition reading as follows:

"If you intend to talk with Padre Pio, please forget about it. His duty is to hear confessions."

When the Padre is about to enter the confessional, there is a roll call of the women who have registered the day before and all line up according to the numbers they have received. (Before these rules were devised there was often great confusion around the confessional, so that more than once the police had to be called in to keep order!)

According to Dr. Festa, who personally observed Padre Pio at table many times in his repeated visits to the monastery, the nourishment he takes is extremely meager. No breakfast. No milk at any time. One meal a day at noon, consisting chiefly of vegetables. Meat or eggs only rarely. Certain meats to be avoided entirely, as well as rice, since they cause indigestion. However, the warm weather days do see the addition of half a glass of beer, or water with a little black coffee added to it. (Lately the beer has been replaced by lemonade.)

Such is the sum total of Padre Pio's daily nourishment. Yet his health is perfect, and he continues his heavy schedule without the least indication of a breakdown.

After a short recreation with the other friars after dinner, the Padre resumes hearing confessions and continues until no more people are to be heard. Anyone who goes to confess to him but tries to cover up or to justify his faults will find a most severe judge—one who will tell him very unceremoniously to leave and to prepare himself better. For Padre Pio wants all

PADRE PIO IN 1950

his penitents to be aware that before God they are guilty, and that they must accuse themselves with sincerity, humility and sorrow.

On many occasions the Padre's habitual kindness is set aside, and people feel most disconcerted at the sudden and rigorous command to leave the confessional. They go, but they experience no peace until they have returned with the proper dispositions. It is then that they find a father again, a giver of peace and joy, so that their confession becomes an unforgettable one. In fact, there is scarcely a person who has gone to confession to Padre Pio who will not admit that "the Padre knew everything I had done, and all the details, too."

For instance, a young lady had come all the way from Brescia to go to confession to Padre Pio. She had made a very careful preparation, and had even written down her sins on a piece of paper. She had hardly started reading her faults, however, when Padre Pio told her to stop and he himself continued their enumeration in the same order in which she had written them.

A society lady, Mrs. Luise Vairo, a baptized Catholic, had abandoned every religious practice and for years had lived outside the Church, concerned only with worldly pleasures. She lived in London, England. A friend of hers had met Padre Pio while on a visit to Italy, and had been so impressed by the experience that, upon his return to London, he could talk of little else.

Her curiosity aroused, Mrs. Vairo decided to go and see Padre Pio, too, and arrived at San Giovanni Rotondo in September, 1925. At that time the town had no comfortable inn, and the road leading to the monastery was broken and stony. To make matters worse, when Mrs. Vairo reached the church of Our Lady of Grace, she felt such a sense of depression, sorrow

79

and grief that she could not contain herself and burst into bitter tears. Her sobs attracted the attention of other women who were in the sacristy talking to Padre Pio. They came to see what was wrong, followed by the Padre.

"Calm yourself, lady, calm yourself," said the friar kindly. "God's mercy is infinite, Jesus died on the cross for sinners."

These were the first words Padre Pio spoke to Mrs. Vairo. Since she intended to leave the same day, she immediately asked if it would not be possible for her to go to confession without delay.

"Come back at three o'clock this afternoon and I will hear your confession," said the Padre. "In the meantime, have some food and rest a while. If you are not going to talk, I will."

At three o'clock, Mrs. Vairo knelt down in Padre Pio's confessional, but now a new surge of emotion made talking almost impossible. Besides, she could not begin to remember the many grievous sins she had committed in the past. Padre Pio was undisturbed, however, and began to tell her exactly what she had done—all her sins and negligences. When he had finished, he asked if she had anything else to add to the list of sins he had just enumerated.

Yes, there was another very serious sin, and Mrs. Vairo well remembered it. But even as she reflected upon it, two voices seemed to clamor within her. One urged her to confess the fault, otherwise her confession would not be complete and valid. The other voice insisted that it was not necessary to confess it, otherwise the Padre would have mentioned this sin as he had mentioned all the others. In the end Mrs. Vairo obeyed the first voice, the right one, and confessed the hidden fault.

"At last!" exclaimed Padre Pio triumphantly. "I was waiting for this!" Then he gave her absolution.

A PROCESSION WITH THE MADONNA

81

This incident was made known by Mrs. Vairo herself, whose conversion continues to be a source of edification to all. For some time she remained in San Giovanni Rotondo, in a house belonging to some women members of the Third Order of Saint Francis, where she undertook such extreme penances that she all but ruined her health. Thus, one winter morning, in wind and sleet, she walked barefoot from the town to the monastery. She reached the church half-frozen, wet to the skin, her feet bleeding, and completely exhausted. As soon as she entered the church she collapsed, and was carried to the sacristy. Here Padre Pio told her that she was going much too rapidly on the way of penance. Then, placing his hand upon her shoulder he remarked with a smile: "One does not get wet with this kind of water," and immediately her clothes became dry.

The penitential spirit of this former idol of society was prompted not only by a desire to atone for her past sins, but also to obtain the conversion of her son. (Like his mother, before coming to Italy, this young man had lost the Faith and never went to church.) Mrs. Vairo wrote frequently to her boy, telling him of her own conversion and of Padre Pio's part in it. All to no avail.

Several months later, however, Mrs. Vairo was coming out of church. A French gentleman had come to see Padre Pio. His car was parked in front of the church. The newcomer offered Mrs. Vairo some French and English newspapers which she began to read with great interest. Then suddenly she uttered a piercing scream. She had just read that the boat on which her son was traveling had been sunk! Although no names were given, fifteen persons were known to be dead and several others injured.

"Who told you that your son was among the dead?" asked

PADRE PIO BAPTIZING ONE OF HIS GREAT-NEPHEWS.

83

Padre Pio, who had come out of the church, with others, at the sound of the poor mother's scream.

"Who assures me that he is safe?" sobbed Mrs. Vairo.

Padre Pio looked up to heaven as though to ask God for some answer to the pathetic question. Then after a moment he smiled, jotted down a few lines on a piece of paper, and handed it to Mrs. Vairo.

"Thank the Lord! Your son is alive and you can reach him at this address," he said. "Don't worry any more."

At once Mrs. Vairo wrote to her son. Then, wonder of wonders! A short time later she received word from him, too, the letters having passed each other on the way.

The son's letter confirmed all that Padre Pio had said. But the boy could not understand how his mother had learned of his new address. As soon as possible he came to San Giovanni Rotondo, was reunited with his mother, went to confession to Padre Pio and returned to the practices of the Faith with real fervor.

Mrs. Vairo now lives near Assisi where the spirit of Saint Francis still abides. We have reported this episode concerning her because it reveals the variety of gifts possessed by Padre Pio, gifts that make his apostolate so efficient and so marvelous.

Padre Pio's actions, especially with insincere and impenitent sinners, may appear to be rude and too severe as, for example, when he closed the slide of the confessional in the face of another English lady who spoke Italian fluently and who had just started her confession. She came out of the confessional crying, and those waiting their turn felt that this time Padre Pio had been too severe. Yet the minister of God's justice did not agree, and he was right. Twenty days later the same lady was praying in church when Padre Pio came up to her.

BENIAMINO GIGLI SINGS FOR PADRE PIO AND FRIENDS IN THE MONASTERY GARDEN, JUNE 20, 1951.

"Do you wish to go to confession?"

"Yes, Father, I have been waiting these twenty days for you to hear me, after you chased me away the other time."

"And do you think that is anything, when Our Lord has waited so long and patiently for you to return, you who have been making sacrilegious Communions all these years?"

Padre Pio made this statement even before the woman entered the confessional—his own way of explaining his former abrupt attitude. However, when the woman sincerely admitted her faults, he showed her the same charity which the Good Shepherd showed to the lost sheep.

Padre Pio does not like repetition, either in the confessional or outside of it. To a lady, unknown to him, who mentioned a sin she had already confessed before, he remarked dryly: "This sin was already forgiven, because you have confessed it twice before, once at the Shrine of Alverna and once at Monte Cassino."

The lady remembered that this was true after Padre Pio had reminded her of it.

This bloody century of wars and destruction has destroyed the peace of mind of millions of people. A man like Padre Pio is a godsend for us all, an instrument of reconciliation, a source of genuine peace. No wonder that the world now runs after him, who had himself run away from the world, and that the mountain solitude appointed for his escape is now populated by hundreds of peace-loving people from every corner of the globe.

Note: It is not necessary to visit the tomb of Padre Pio to experience his help in any need. This may be considered true in a special way by all members of the Blue Army whom Father Pio adopted as his "special children", and also of all Franciscans.

Chapter Twelve

The Voice of Prophecy and Bilocation

PROPHECY means primarily the power and the authority to speak in God's Name, and secondarily to confirm the teaching by an accurate foretelling of future events which cannot be known in a natural way. Padre Pio not only possesses the power to read minds and to know the past other than by natural means, the future itself is often clearly revealed to him. This may account for the fact that recently some dire predictions of things to come—days of darkness, fire and destruction—circulated by misguided persons and falsely attributed to Padre Pio, were believed by many because of the Padre's well-known power of prophecy. At the time a formal denial was issued in his name, since he had never made such statements.

There are many reports of authentic prophecies made by the Padre. They come from people to whom, or in whose favor, such predictions were made. A few of these, chosen because of the reliability of their informative sources, are given here.

Young Dr. Franco Lotti of Bologna, acquainted with Padre Pio since childhood, states that during World War II he had been assigned to a regiment stationed in Greece. Early in July, 1943, he obtained a furlough and spent most of it with Padre Pio in San Giovanni Rotondo. Finally came the day of departure, and he went to say good-bye to his good friend. Suddenly he noticed that Padre Pio was looking at him in a strange, almost anxious manner.

"I hope I'm not going to be given a medal *in memoriam,*" said the young doctor jokingly.

Padre Pio hesitated, then shook his head. "No, that won't happen to you. But—well, what's your destination?"

"Greece, Father."

Again Padre Pio shook his head. "No, you're not going to Greece," he declared, and with such conviction that the young doctor was most impressed. However, he returned to his base in northern Italy, according to orders, and there was told that all the necessary documents for his departure for Greece would be ready the following Monday.

Monday came, and instead of receiving his documents, Dr. Lotti was told to wait for further instructions. His departure for Greece was now fixed for July 25, 1943. But on that day Mussolini's dictatorship came to a sudden and dramatic end, and the Fascists were overthrown. Now the necessity for keeping troops at home for the protection of the new government made it impossible to send help elsewhere. So Dr. Lotti never went to Greece, just as Padre Pio had foretold.[1]

The friar's prophecy that a Capuchin monastery would be built in Pietrelcina was referred to in an earlier chapter. This prophecy was made at a time when Padre Pio had no apparent basis for issuing such a statement. Yet in February, 1947, the Sacred Congregation for Religious granted the Capuchins permission to open a house of their Order in Pietrelcina. In July they took possession of it, and on May 20, 1951, the public church was completed and solemnly dedicated.

Another promise of a prophetic nature is connected with the erection of this same monastery. The town of Pietrelcina has

---

[1] *Padre Pio da Pietrelcina,* by Dr. Franco Lotti, p. 20 f.

very little water. The builders, handicapped by this situation, decided to ask Padre Pio for help. When he had been shown the blueprint, he placed his finger on a certain spot.

"Dig five meters from here and you will find all the water you need," he said.

At this time Padre Pio was in San Giovanni Rotondo, a considerable distance from Pietrelcina. The workers had already probed for water many times in the vicinity of the new monastery, always without result. Now, however, digging at the exact place suggested by Padre Pio, they found a splendid supply. Today, this not only serves the monastery but also part of the town.

One day the local police chief went to see Padre Pio, accompanied by his wife who was expecting a child. The couple asked their good friend what name they should give their little one.

"Call him Pio," said the friar, smiling.

"But what if it's a girl?"

"I told you to call him Pio," replied the Padre emphatically. And Pio was the name the happy parents gave their child— a boy!

Two years later the police chief again approached Padre Pio with a similar request.

"Call him Francis."

"But Padre—"

"Man of little faith!" said the friar warningly.

This time the baby was also a boy, and of course he received the name of Francis.

L. C., of Castel del Rio (Bologna) was requested by two local families to ask Padre Pio about their sons, missing in

World War II. A returning veteran had reported one of them as dead. The bad news was kept from the boy's mother, although the rest of the family knew about it. Padre Pio's answer regarding this "dead" soldier was simple and to the point:

"In good health, and there are good hopes. He will return home in a few months."

Those who had heard of the lad's death were skeptical, despite Padre Pio's promise. When two months had passed without any further news, they were even more so. Then, at the end of the third month, the "dead" soldier suddenly arrived from France, very much alive and in good health.

The other boy was working in Germany and for a long time had not sent any news of himself to his people.

"He, too, will return soon," said Padre Pio. One month later he was back.

When Italian towns were being bombed by Allied planes at the beginning of World War II, the people of San Giovanni Rotondo begged Padre Pio to intercede for them with God, their town being so close to the strategic air base of Foggia.

"Your town won't be touched," declared Padre Pio emphatically.

These words proved true. Not a single bomb ever fell on San Giovanni Rotondo, even though many Allied planes flew over it. Soldiers came, but on a peaceful mission. Later they came as pilgrims and penitents of Padre Pio.

It is reported that when certain Allied fliers were about to drop bombs on San Giovanni Rotondo, they saw the figure of a friar with protecting arms extended over it. This vision so unnerved the airmen that they flew on without releasing any bombs.[2]

---

[2] *Padre Pio da Pietrelcina,* by Piera Delfino Sessa, p. 11.

Many of Padre Pio's prophecies are connected with miraculous cures. For instance, a seven-year-old girl of Ribera (Agrigento), Gemma Di Giorgi by name, was blind since birth. There were no pupils in her eyes. Her grandmother decided to visit Padre Pio and ask him to pray that the little one would be cured. She also decided to take the youngster with her, so that the poor child might go to confession and receive her first Holy Communion from the hands of Padre Pio.

After hearing Gemma's confession, Padre Pio gently touched her sightless eyes and assured the grandmother that all would be well.

"Your granddaughter will be able to see," he declared earnestly. "I'm sure of that."

True enough. The little girl received her sight soon after making her First Communion, despite the fact that her eyes were still without pupils. This extraordinary cure, and the prophecy preceding it, aroused enormous interest in the Italian press during the summer of 1947.[3]

To another afflicted parent who had come to San Giovanni Rotondo to ask for a cure for his son, who was both blind and paralyzed, Padre Pio was equally helpful.

"Go home, and your boy will be cured and able to see you," he said.

The parent obeyed, and upon his arrival at home he found his son seeing and well again.

In his humility, Padre Pio often excuses himself when people ask for information on soldiers missing in action, or made prisoners of war.

---

[3] This rare case is not the first one of its kind. The annals of the miraculous cures at Lourdes report the case of Mrs. Bire, on August 5, 1908. She, too, received her sight, even though her eyes remained without pupils.

"How could I know anything about that?" he will say.

However, such evasive answers generally mean that he does not wish to be "the angel of affliction" and give bad news to the relatives. At other times he may exclaim "God's Will be done!" thus preparing family or friends for the inevitable sorrow.

At all times his desire is to comfort the afflicted. "There is a ray of hope," he may say occasionally, which means that the person in question is still alive but in great difficulty.

Some ten days before the Italian election of April 18, 1948, when many Catholics were greatly worried about the outcome of the campaign between the Communists and the Christian Democrats, Padre Pio told a group of pilgrims not to be alarmed.

"Our Lady and the prayers of our Holy Father will save us," he said.

We also feel that his own prayers contributed to the victory of the Christian Democrats, thus saving both Italy and the Vatican from Stalin's domination.

The extraordinary phenomenon of bilocation means that an individual is present in two different places at the same time. We read of this phenomenon having taken place in the lives of certain saints—i.e., Saint Anthony of Padua and Saint Alphonsus Liguori. We know the facts, but their explanation remains a mystery similar to many other wonders in the mystical life.

One day a friar was discussing bilocation in the presence of Padre Pio.

"Perhaps the saints are not aware of the phenomenon when it takes place," he said.

But Padre Pio shook his head emphatically. "Oh, yes, they're aware of it. They may be in doubt as to whether the body or soul goes, but they know very well what takes place, and they know where they are going."

Padre Pio was actually speaking from experience. He has never left San Giovanni Rotondo since his arrival there in December, 1917, and yet he has been seen in towns hundreds of miles away, in Rome, and even in Uruguay. One may well be tempted to explain these appearances as mere illusions or hallucinations on the part of those who report them, but often these persons are entirely above suspicion and have something very concrete by which to prove their statements.

The late Monsignor D'Indico of Florence reported that his sister was dying of typhus, despite the best of medical care. On July 20, 1921, she was in a coma. The Monsignor was alone in his office when suddenly he felt that someone was standing behind him. He looked around and saw a friar who suddenly disappeared.

The prelate left his office and met one of his chaplains to whom he related the strange experience. The chaplain thought it was all a matter of hallucination, because of the prelate's concern about his sister's serious condition. However, when they both called to see the sick woman, they found that she was no longer in a coma but completely out of danger. Even more surprising, she told them that a friar had come into her room and spoken to her.

"Don't be afraid," he had said. "Your fever will disappear tomorrow, and in a few days no trace of your sickness will be left."

"But Father, you must be a saint!"

"No, I am a creature whom the Lord uses for His mercies."

"Please let me kiss your habit, Father!"

"No, kiss these marks of the Passion instead," said the unknown visitor, and showed her his wounded and bleeding hands. Then, after a few more words, he blessed her and disappeared.

All this took place in Florence on July 20, 1921. The relatives of the sick woman had written to Padre Pio several days before, asking for his prayers. The dying lady immediately felt better, her fever disappearing the following morning as Padre Pio had promised. A week later she was completely cured.

The Padre's bilocated presence always leaves something to prove its reality. In this case we have not only the word of the sick person herself, but also that of her brother, a prelate of the Church.

Padre Pio has always had a great admiration for Pope Pius X, recently beatified by Pope Pius XII. He insists that Pius X is the most lovable of all the Popes since the time of Saint Peter, so much like Jesus in his humility and simplicity. Several persons worthy of belief have testified that they saw Padre Pio praying before the tomb of Pius X in the crypt of the Basilica of Saint Peter, where the body lay before the ceremonies of beatification. These rumors were reported to Pope Pius XI, who asked the late saintly priest, Don Orione, if he had ever seen Padre Pio praying in the Basilica.

"Yes, I have seen him there," answered Don Orione.

"Well, now that you confirm these rumors, I also believe," replied the Pope.

Padre Pio was in Rome by bilocation more than once. It is reported that he brought a relic of the Holy Cross to the Eternal City without leaving San Giovanni Rotondo. He presented it to a young nun there, telling her to give it to Countess Virginia

Sili (a sister-in-law of Cardinal Sili), early that morning before the dedication of the new chapel in her palace at Via del Tritone 53, Rome. A few days later Countess Virginia went to see Padre Pio in San Giovanni Rotondo, and from him she learned that the sacred relic had been brought to Rome by bilocation.

The Capuchin Father who had given the relic to Padre Pio confirmed the truth of this extraordinary occurrence.

Mrs. Concetta Bellarmini of San Vito Lanciano was desperately ill, and a relative advised her to ask Padre Pio for help. She did so, despite the opposition of her sons who were chemists. She had never met Padre Pio but one day she saw a stigmatized friar standing in the center of the room where she lay sick in bed. He smiled at her, then gave her his blessing.

Mrs. Bellarmini was not alarmed at this strange occurrence. On the contrary, a great calm came over her, and she felt impelled to ask the friar if his coming meant her own recovery or some blessing for her children.

"Next Sunday morning you will be well again," said the friar. Then he disappeared, leaving behind an unusual fragrance which was also noticed by the maid.

To the great surprise of doctors and relatives, Mrs. Bellarmini was immediately and completely cured by the following Sunday. Soon she was on her way to San Giovanni Rotondo. When she saw Padre Pio there, surrounded by a devout throng of laity and religious, she became very excited.

"Yes, there he is!" she cried. "He's the one!"

A number of similar happenings are reported by Del Fante and other biographers of Padre Pio. They remark that occasionally his presence becomes manifest at a great distance by his characteristic perfume, or his voice, or they are warned by other means than bilocation. Sometimes, too, people perceive him in dreams. That these are not ordinary dreams, produced by the subconscious mind or by fantasy, is evidenced by their extraordinary results. For instance, the conversion of Italia Betti, already described, had its beginning in a dream wherein she saw Padre Pio showing her what she must do in order to obtain peace.

Yes, since 1917 Padre Pio has been relegated to a distant corner on the spur of the boot of the Italian peninsula. In all these years he has never left his humble mountain retreat, or known any other home than his Cell in the Monastery of Our Lady of Grace. But who can prevent the Spirit of God from taking his voice, his aura, his second bilocated self throughout the world? Who can prevent the love of this saintly man from extending far beyond the confines of his monastery?

Once or twice during his past thirty years Padre Pio's superiors did decide to transfer him to an unknown destination. In this way, they reasoned, they would end the annoyance caused by crowds flocking to the monastery, and their uncontrollable admiration for the Padre. But the news leaked out. Or perhaps the people sensed it instinctively. At any rate, everyone in San Giovanni Rotondo was alerted and mobilized for night and day watch about the monastery. At all costs, the townsfolk were resolved to keep Padre Pio with them. This state of affairs continued until official assurance was given that the Padre would remain where he was.

Note: An entire book might be written about the controversies which surrounded Padre Pio throughout his life. They were the occasion of great suffering to him and to all who loved him. The devil who took even the form of his own spiritual advisor to dissuade him from some of his holy practices also took many forms in trying to prevent the wave of holiness which flowed from Father Pio to all who approached him and to all the world.

In the presence of Cardinal Meyer of Chicago (now deceased), and of several priests who accompanied a Blue Army pilgrimage to San Giovanni, Father Pio made this prophecy:

"Russia will be converted when there is a Blue Army member for every Communist."

Once a woman from Paris asked of Father Pio if she should learn Russian so she might volunteer to go to Russia one day to help the restoration of religion. Father Pio said she could but with a gesture of impatience asked: "But when will Russia open her doors?" (SOUL Magazine, July 1960, pg. 18). Father Pio discouraged fears of an atomic war and encouraged hope in the peace promised by Our Lady of Fatima. "Is there not our Heavenly MAMA," he asked. "Why should we no longer have confidence in her?"

AT PRAYER IN 1962

Chapter Thirteen

The Voice of the Mountain

THE huge promontory known as Mount Gargano dominates the vast rolling plains of Apulia and the Adriatic Sea. It is the highest mountain in this section of the peninsula, Mount Calvo being 3,158 feet in height and Mount Nero 3,033 feet. These imposing mountain peaks are wild and beautiful, particularly in the vicinity of the pine forest of San Menaio. The vegetation is especially rich in the highlands, where oak, beech and pine trees abound. Holm oak and chestnut trees grow farther down, and in the valleys, while olive trees are to be found near the base of the mountain where the vegetation is not so rich.

The plains around Gargano are extremely fertile, the vineyards producing some of the finest wines in all Italy. The town of San Giovanni Rotondo, which today has 15,000 inhabitants, is located on a plateau midway between the peaks of Mount Nero and Mount Calvo, on the southern side of the promontory.

Mount Gargano has been a sacred place since the days of Pope Gelasius (492-496), when the glorious Prince of the heavenly hosts, Saint Michael the Archangel, appeared in a cave on the mountainside and revealed to the local Bishop that the mountain was under his protection for the honor of God and of the Holy Angels. The cave where this apparition took place was subsequently turned into a shrine, and is only a few miles from San Giovanni Rotondo, on the road to Foggia. The place is now called Saint Angelo.

Mount Gargano has been a place of pilgrimage since the end of the fifth century. Countless numbers have come here to pray, including Francis of Assisi, the first saint to be stigmatized. In fact, it was on September 17, 1224, during his forty days' fast on Mount Alverna in honor of Saint Michael, that Francis received the stigmata. (He had been fasting and praying almost continuously since the Feast of the Assumption in order to prepare himself worthily for the solemn observance of Saint Michael's feast on September 29.)

The great devotion of the Little Poor Man of Assisi to Saint Michael, and his visit to the shrine at Mount Gargano, are elements which Divine Providence has now joined into one picture, despite an interlude of seven centuries. For Padre Pio is a son of Saint Francis, and he also received his mystical seal in September, a few days before the feast of Saint Michael.

Padre Pio's devotion to the great Archangel consists not only of prayer and penance but also of direct attacks against the devil. In this he imitates those blessed spirits of the faithful heavenly armies in the endless struggle against Satan. When he came to live in the Gargano region, he came to his headquarters, as it were—to the mountain chosen by Saint Michael —who, in these days of great apostasy and diabolical iniquity, seems to be regrouping his human allies—saintly souls and apostles—for the great struggle. No better place could have been assigned to Padre Pio than this monastery on the slope of Mount Gargano, where his mission receives the support and protection of the glorious Prince of the heavenly hosts.

One day some of Padre Pio's penitents were talking about diabolical vexations.

"My hand will crush the devil!" declared the Padre emphatically.

Saint Michael himself must have inspired this courageous utterance. Certainly it was not a mere gesture, or connected with wishful thinking. Indeed, the sacristy where the good friar administers the Sacrament of Penance and the confessional in the church itself where the women kneel before him are actually twin battlefields. Here, times without number, the devil goes down to ignominious defeat, and those whom he would have kept in dismal slavery are once again made children of God and soldiers of Jesus Christ.

A more manifest sign of Padre Pio's extraordinary power over Satan is to be found in the various cases of possession in which he has exorcised the devil by a single word of command. Thus, during the month of September, 1947, a poor Italian woman, manifestly possessed by the Evil One, was taken by her sons to San Giovanni Rotondo to see Padre Pio. The boys actually had to use physical force to get their mother to enter the church where Padre Pio was in the act of offering Mass. But as soon as she was inside, the poor woman let out such screams that everyone was terrified. (For years she had acted in this manner whenever she saw a church, a crucifix or a sacred picture.)

When Padre Pio began to distribute Holy Communion, things became even worse for then the woman burst into curses and blasphemies.

"Take her out of here!" ordered Padre Pio finally.

At this the obsessed woman began to struggle furiously. "I'd rather die than go out!" she screamed.

Solemnly raising the sacred Host over the ciborium, Padre Pio fixed her with a stern glance.

"It is time now to put an end to this," he said. At these words, the possessed woman fell to the floor as though dead. But she was not dead, for presently she got to her feet and walked to a corner of the church where she sat down quietly, free at last from the tyrannical possession of Satan. Since that memorable day she has paid frequent visits to San Giovanni Rotondo, and has told countless people of her good fortune and of Padre Pio's extraordinary power over the devil.

"He is more powerful than Saint Michael," she insists—an exaggeration that is quite forgivable.

Father Alexander Lingua writes that on a pilgrimage from northern Italy to San Giovanni Rotondo (September 27-October 3, 1950), he met a similar case—a possessed woman from the city of Prato. She had been taken along on the pilgrimage in the hope that Padre Pio would be able to free her from the devil's power.

When the group arrived at Loreto, they paid the usual visit to Our Lady's famous shrine. But not a quiet visit, for the demoniac caused a terrible commotion in the Basilica and in the Holy House by her dreadful screams. Various measures were employed to calm her, but without success. Yet the following morning, when taken to Padre Pio and blessed by him, the devil immediately left her. At dinner that same day she sat at table with Father Lingua, perfectly calm and extremely happy. She took this opportunity to inform the priest that for eighteen years she had been unable to enter a church—the devil tormenting her more severely than usual whenever she tried to do so. But all this was over now, thanks to Padre Pio's blessing.

The frail young Capuchin who came to San Giovanni Rotondo so many years ago, to recover his health or to die, has indeed shown himself an able soldier of Christ, a champion par excellence in the glorious army of Saint Michael the Archangel.

There is another voice that comes from the mountain dedicated to Saint Michael. This is the voice of the Monastery of

Our Lady of Grace, whose entire history seems to be a kind of preparation for the arrival of Padre Pio and the great work of charity he has recently inaugurated.

Some ten years after the foundation of the Capuchin Order by Father Matteo da Bascio, early in the sixteenth century, the residents of San Giovanni Rotondo (at that time numbering scarcely two thousand) decided to erect a monastery and church in honor of Our Lady of Grace on a barren mountain slope about two miles beyond the town. Having obtained permission for this from their Bishop, who later became Pope Julius III, they chose the newly-established Capuchin Order to take charge of the project.

The first friars arrived at the town in 1540, and erected an iron cross in front of the monastery site which is still standing today. Unfortunately political and economic difficulties interfered with the proposed work, so that the church was not opened for worship until 1616.

The history of both church and monastery reflects the history and the spirit of the Capuchin Order itself. For years the friars had no other revenue save from what they could produce on a piece of land donated to them, part of which is now the monastery garden. The rest had to be supplied by begging. Indeed, from the very beginning the life of the Capuchins at San Giovanni Rotondo was one of real poverty and sacrifice. Yet Divine Providence never failed them, and the monastery annals report some extraordinary facts to prove God's predilection for these faithful followers of Saint Francis.

Thus, during one very cold winter, the snow on the mountain slope was so deep that it was impossible for anyone to go out to beg for food. Nor could the townsfolk get supplies to the monastery. As a result, the friars' larder was soon bare. Yet they continued to fulfill all their religious duties, trusting that God would take care of them.

For several days the snow fell without interruption. Almost on the verge of starvation, the community was praying fervently for help when suddenly four strange young men knocked at the gate. Each carried a large quantity of provisions which they graciously presented to the friars. But when asked who they were, the newcomers smiled and shook their heads.

"Thank the Lord, Who never abandons His children who trust in Him," they said, and disappeared.

When the storm had abated and once again it became possible to reach the town, the friars made every effort to discover the identity of their benefactors. All to no avail. And since no trace of footsteps could be found in the snow, all were finally convinced that it was four angels in human form who had come to their rescue.

It would be impossible to list all the saintly men who have served God in the Monastery of Our Lady of Grace. However, mention should be made of Saint Camillus de Lellis, who after his conversion in 1575, entered upon his novitiate here as a Capuchin. Eventually, however, a very serious sickness forced him to leave. When he ventured a second attempt at religious life, a return of his former affliction made him realize that heaven had other designs for him. So, resigned to God's Will, he left the monastery and in due course discovered his life's work.

With the suppression of religious communities and the expropriation of Church property by the civil government, in the second half of the nineteenth century, the Monastery of Our Lady of Grace became a victim of secularization. The Capuchin community there was suppressed, although one friar did manage to remain behind as custodian. Then in 1865 the monastery was turned into a home for the sick poor. It served in this capacity until 1909, when the Capuchins were permitted to return to Our Lady of Grace and resume their lives of prayer and penance.

With the arrival of Padre Pio, in December, 1917, a new era began—not only for the monastery but also for the town of San Giovanni Rotondo. Gradually the sacred mountain became a place of pilgrimage once again, so that today visitors number into the thousands, and include Cardinals, Bishops, priests, and men and women outstanding in all walks of life.

Among the many celebrities who have visited Padre Pio in recent years are two idols of the Italian stage—Carlo Companini and Erminio Macario. Better known to world audiences is another visitor, the great Italian tenor Beniamino Gigli, who arrived at the Monastery of Our Lady of Grace on June 20, 1951. Late in the afternoon of that same day, Signor Gigli entertained the Padre and some of his friends in the seclusion of the monastery garden. Here, surrounded by stately cypress and amid a profusion of lilies and roses, the famous operatic tenor related some of the interesting experiences of his career. Then he sang several songs. The first of these was *Ninna nanna,* a cradle song. Then followed some Neapolitan folk songs, which Padre Pio seemed to enjoy especially. (He himself speaks the Neapolitan dialect.) Finally, with great emotion, Gigli sang *Mamma!*

This touching air found an echo in the heart of every listener, but especially in that of Padre Pio. Surrounded by his friends, his eyes lowered, his whole being attentive, the friar seemed to be carried out of himself at the sound of Gigli's golden voice. No doubt he was thinking of his own dear mother lying still in death not far away from that same monastery garden. At any rate, when the song was over, he found it hard to face his friends and to thank the great artist for his kindness, for his eyes were filled with tears.

Before leaving, Signor Gigli promised to return at a future date and to contribute to Padre Pio's special charity which we shall discuss presently: *The Home for the Relief of Suffering.*

Padre Pio's mother, who died on January 3, 1929, is no longer alone in the cemetery of San Giovanni Rotondo. Her faithful husband was also laid to rest there on October 6, 1946. For when advancing age found Zi' Orazio unable to work the little farm near Pietrelcina, he decided to spend his last days close to his beloved son.

For nearly six years he lived as the guest of Mary Pyle (formerly of New York City) in a house close to the Capuchin monastery. Naturally the most solemn moments of the old man's days occurred every morning when he attended Padre Pio's Mass and received Holy Communion from his stigmatized hands. He was also allowed to share the meals of the Capuchin community, which afforded him particular satisfaction, inasmuch as later he had the opportunity to talk briefly with Padre Pio whom crowds of pilgrims were always clamoring to see.

Zi' Orazio spent many hours of each day sitting under the old elm tree before the church of Our Lady of Grace, gladly engaging in conversation with visitors. In his picturesque dialect he would recall episodes of Padre Pio's early life, with an abundance of minute details, as well as anecdotes of his own days in Pietrelcina and America. However, after some years he became too feeble to walk to church. Then loyal friends procured a little donkey for him, and by this means he continued to go to Mass every morning. But in the fall of 1946 he took seriously ill and began to fail rapidly. When he died, on October 5, Padre Pio was on hand to assist him and to prepare his soul to appear before God.

"Tata mio, tata mio!" cried the Padre, now orphaned of both parents, but bravely offering to the Heavenly Father this long-expected sorrow.

Chapter Fourteen

The Voice of Padre Pio

PADRE PIO does not preach sermons. However, by his example he preaches with more eloquence and efficacy than the greatest of sacred orators, especially in the confessional. There was even a time when he directed souls by mail, imparting to them that light and wisdom which the Holy Spirit had bestowed upon him. Then came the period when people were forbidden to write to him and he himself immediately put an end to all correspondence. Today, though such restrictions no longer exist, Padre Pio still considers himself bound by obedience and writes to no one.

The letters which do exist, written by him to his spiritual children, date from the years immediately preceding or following his stigmatization. In a striking manner they reveal his soul's deep spirituality and mystical elevation during this period of time. The wise counsels imparted by him in the confessional or on other occasions, and recorded by his spiritual children, are now considered most precious documents. At present such material is little more than fragmentary. Therefore, we shall give only a few excerpts from his letters and spiritual advice, translating directly from the original.

FROM HIS LETTERS

". . . Do not worry about taking my time, because we cannot spend our time in a better manner than in leading souls to sanctity. I myself do not know how to thank our Heavenly Father for His kindness in bringing me souls whom I can help a little.

"Oh, how I wish that God had been pleased to let me spend all my life in this sacred ministry! I, on the contrary, have wasted my time in offending God, and by my bad example I have stolen from Jesus souls whom He had redeemed with His Blood. In this I have been far worse than Lucifer. I know well that nobody is spotless before the Lord, but my own uncleanness is without parallel. Such is the deformity of my soul that when I think of it my sacred habit seems to be horrified at my filth. And yet the kindness of the God of our Fathers is ever ready, and He has never excluded my soul from His mercy...."

"... Walk with simplicity in the way of the Lord and do not torment your spirit.... Learn to hate your faults, but with calm.... And if the devil makes a great deal of noise about you, rejoice, for this is a good sign. What we must dread is his peace and his harmony with the human soul...."

"... My dearest daughters and sisters, this is no abandonment but love that our sweetest Saviour is showing you. It is not at all true that you offend Him, for His watchful grace keeps you from doing so. It is also not true that you need a general confession of the sins of your past life, as some of you seem to believe. You well know how often we have discussed this matter, and how far from reality is your way of thinking. From these letters of yours, and from the many occasions I have had of meeting you personally, I have come to the conclusion that the state of your souls, even though not all in the same manner, is undoubtedly one of desolation, or of spiritual suffering of a sacred nature. Specifically I assure you again in the Lord:

"1. The darkness that sometimes covers the sky of your souls is nothing but light. You imagine yourselves to be in the dark, and in the midst of the burning bush. As a matter of fact, whenever the bush is afire the surrounding air is darkened by smoke. The frightened spirit is then afraid of not being able to see or to understand anything any more. But it is exactly then that God speaks, and that He is present in the soul which listens, understands, loves and trembles. Courage, my daughters! Do not wait to come to Mount Tabor to see God; you are contemplating Him on Mount Sinai. This, I think, is not a case of disturbance and indisposition of your spiritual appetite that prevents you from tasting the sweetness of spiritual goods; it is, rather, an inability to taste anything outside the Supreme Good in Himself. Hence comes that feeling of dissatisfaction with everything that is not God.

"2. The knowledge of your own unworthiness and deformity is a most pure divine light whereby you are forced to reflect on your own nature and its potentiality for every sort of crime, and it was granted to the greatest saints because it both protects the soul from every feeling of pride and vanity and increases humility, which is the basis of true virtue and of Christian perfection. Saint Teresa herself had this knowledge, and she says that at times it brought with it enough pain and horror to cause death, if the Lord had not sustained her.

"3. The knowledge of our own potential unworthiness, of which we have been speaking, should not be mistaken for the knowledge of our actual unworthiness. The former renders the creature dear and acceptable before the Most High; the latter renders her detestable because it is a reflex of sin and iniquity actually present in the soul and on the conscience. In the darkness in which you find yourselves at present, you confuse the one with the other, and from the knowledge of what you might be you fear that you are actually so.

"4. Not to know whether you are worthy of love or of hatred before God is a trial and not a punishment, because one is not afraid of being unworthy when he wants to be so and actually is so. God permits this uncertainty in all people in order that there be no presumption on their part and that they may act with great caution in the business of their eternal salvation. In your particular case, God allows it in order that in this torment you may find your cross and its reward. If you were always sure of God's love, would you be able to suffer any longer? What pain and what merit could then be found in your souls possessed of such a conviction? The most cruel torments would then be roses. What should comfort you is the authoritative voice of him who guides you. You should not care to see yourselves clearly. This is not necessary. It is enough that he who directs you and takes care of your souls has a clear vision of what you are. Believe what you are told; it does not matter whether your spirit must be bent to do so. The martyrs themselves had to believe in the midst of suffering. The most beautiful act of faith is the one we make while we are in darkness, the one we make with sacrifice, and with a violent effort.

"5. Even the lack of complete resignation and the rebellion you seem to experience in the midst of these desolations are tests. The spirit surrenders, but the lower nature rebels and you think that the spirit also has rebelled. Believe me, this cannot happen.

"6. God can reject everything in a creature that was conceived in sin and that carries the unfortunate mark of sin inherited from Adam, but He is absolutely unable to reject our sincere wish to love Him. Therefore, if for other reasons you feel that you cannot be sure of His Heavenly Mercy, and you refuse to believe in the assurances I give you in our sweetest Lord, you must at least feel assured by your sincere desire to love God. In conclusion, you should be at peace—happy that God is satisfied with you, and that He finds in you His restful abode. Temptations, discouragement, disquietude, etc., are all merchandise offered by the devil but rejected; therefore, no harm in all this. Remember that as long as the devil makes a great noise, he is still on the outside and has not yet entered. What we must fear is his peaceful harmony with the human soul. Believe me, for I am talking to you as a brother, and with the authority of a priest who is your spiritual director. Expel from yourselves all these vain fears; break the dark clouds which the devil is placing about your souls in order to torment you and, if possible, to keep you away from your daily Communion. I know that the Lord allows the enemy to make these assaults in order that His Mercy may render you dear to Himself. He wants you to resemble Him in the agonies of the desert, of the Garden of Olives, and of the Cross. But you must defend yourselves by driving the devil away and despising all his evil insinuations. Have I made myself clear? And now I pause because I cannot go on. Let me know if you need anything else, and pray for me always with a holy importunity, especially for the granting of that grace of which I have told you. As for me, in my prayers I remember all of you and all those other souls that are united with us in one spirit before Jesus. . . .

Your Humble Servant,

F. Pio, Cappno."[1]

---

[1] The above letter was written in Padre Pio's native Pietrelcina on the

"... The most beautiful *Credo* is the one we pronounce when we are in darkness, in the hour of sacrifice and sorrow, in the supreme effort of an inflexible will for what is good. This is the one that as a flash of lightning breaks the darkness of the soul; the one that in the midst of a raging storm lifts up the soul and leads it to God.... The prayers of the saints in heaven and of good souls here on earth are a perfume which is never lost. Take care that the sad spectacle of human injustice may not disturb your soul, for this, too, has its place in the general economy. It is upon this human injustice that one day we shall see the Justice of God rise infallibly in triumph."

———

"... May Jesus console, sustain and bless you always, and may He make you taste the sweetness of what He says in His Gospel: 'My yoke is sweet and My burden light.' I leave it to you to realize how welcome your letter has been to me: God be always thanked and blessed for it! I thank you, too, for your very kind words of appreciation in my regard. But you, in all truth, must know that I myself do not deserve any praise or thanks because whatever good is in me is God's work and whatever wickedness is in me is my work. My dear lady, I of myself can do only one thing, commit sin, and then ... nothing more than new sins."

———

eve of the feast of the Immaculate Conception, 1916. It was addressed, like several other extant letters, to those members of the Third Order of Saint Francis whom he was guiding to Christian perfection. When Padre Pio wrote this letter, and the ones which follow, he was about to leave for military service in Naples. It seems that the grace he expected his spiritual daughters to obtain for him was that of being spared the great trial of exchanging his religious habit for a soldier's uniform.

December 10, 1914

J. M. J.

"Peace, mercy and grace be with you always, and with all those who love Our Lord Jesus Christ in all sincerity! Amen.

"I wrote you a long time ago, and to this day I have received no reply. What is the reason? Knowing your superlative diligence and extreme courtesy, I cannot help being worried at your silence.

"I hope that God's infinite Mercy will allow me to hear that it was only because of your many duties that you did not find time to send me word about yourself and thus forget him who constantly sends up prayers and thanksgiving to the Heavenly Father for you. I am waiting impatiently for your letter in order to obtain exact information regarding your whole family, especially the most precious Giovina, to whose prayers, as to yours and Rosina's, I recommend the life of my soul.

"I was told that you were getting better, and I must confess that I was greatly pleased to hear that. But now, not having received any letter from you, I am very sad and worried for the doubt comes to mind that perhaps I have been deceived this time. Besides, a few days ago the Lord permitted me to pay a visit to Giovina, and by means of me our dear Jesus showered many graces upon her on that occasion. At that time it seemed to me that her health was better than in the past. I am worrying about this, too. Enlighten me about everything in your letter. But, please, no word to Giovina about my visit there. (It is good to hide the secret of a King.)[2]

---

[2] There is an element of mystery in this letter. Padre Pio speaks of a visit made by God's favor to the sick Giovina. He was there, saw her, saw the graces she received, but he asks the addressee not to tell Giovina of his visit. Had he been there by bilocation and invisibly? The quotation from Tobias, 12:7, about the King's secret, seems to confirm our inter-

". . . Do not call me importunate if I show myself quite solicitous and anxious about your salvation. You must remember that I have espoused you to Jesus, and I am jealous and afraid that others may ensnare you. Please remember that I have assumed a serious obligation to watch over you, an obligation which forces me to keep away from you every pestiferous breath in order to present you as a chaste virgin to the Divine Spouse when He shall come to ask for you again. Woe unto me if I fail my obligation!"

December 12, 1914

J. M. J.

"May the Father of Our Lord Jesus Christ fill you always with His grace, and render you an ever worthier spouse of His Divine Son! Amen.

"Our letters met and greeted each other on the way. I am surprised at the delay of your long awaited letter. Satan had his foot in this business, trying to divert this letter of yours, but praised be the Immaculate Virgin Mary who did not permit this to happen. Another great defeat, this one, for that ugly creature the devil. I cannot tell you how much my heart rejoices, in the midst of my miseries, in hearing about your good health and that of Giovina. May the Lord continue to show mercy to us, and to comfort us in all the events of this present life! I am really unable to tell you how grateful I am to such a good Father for the many blessings He showers upon us continuously, regardless of our unworthiness, especially mine, which has now

---

pretation. The fact is that many reports of ecstatic flights and invisible visits to distant places are circulated today about Padre Pio. This letter seems to confirm those rumors. The date would prove that such gifts were possessed by him years before he was stigmatized.

reached the limit. To Him be eternal praise and honor from all His creatures. I can scarcely find words to thank you for the prayers and the novenas that you are offering for me to Our Lady of Pompeii, being aware of my own inability to do so. May Jesus reward you for everything.

"While I must admire your sincerity in telling me that you do not feel able to ask the Divine Spouse of our souls to break the ties that keep me united to this body, I cannot help telling you that such news is like a sword that cuts through my heart, increasing my agony. Now, why deny me this favor? I will not call you cruel, because you have been sincere with me, but by the loving-kindness of God Incarnate, try to do it in the future, otherwise you will become an assassin. I shall be all alone then in praying for this intention. I shall never be heard, possessing a heart that is filthy with sin and a tongue that is sacrilegious to the extreme!"

J. M. J.

"With unsteady hand I am trying to write these few lines. Only yesterday I returned from Morcone where in a very few days my condition became extremely low. Now more than ever I feel the pleasure that comes from this new trial which Jesus has sent me. I have become very thin and emaciated, weak in the extreme. I can scarcely stand, and I fear that the Lord may repay me in this life. Pray to Jesus Who has been pleased to test His servant with fire! . . . You, too, my dearest sister, thank the infinite Mercy of the Lord for not having allowed our enemy to touch my spirit in this extreme trial, despite my unworthiness. How sweet it is to live in the shadow of the Lord in the sacred cloister! Perhaps I am unworthy to rest within those holy precincts, and that is why the Lord almost forcibly tries to expel me.

"His Will be done, Who wishes to put the loyalty of His servant to an extreme test! At my loss, the Lord seems to hear the prayers of these devout people who want me to remain among them at any cost. This is not just my impression. No, they have shown it on various occasions, especially on my last return home. When I entered the town, they came out thanking the Lord and shouting *'Evviva!'* because of my return. I was moved to tears. I tremble, however, at the thought that the Lord may reward me in this life. Pray to Jesus, pray that He may keep my reward for the life to come.

"You tell me that you are afraid of your own weakness and you want to know what to do to get rid of it. Humble yourself before the Lord, and do not be afraid of anything. Your weakness is not such as to be displeasing to the Divine Lover. Pray to the most loving Jesus that He may dispel from you unnecessary fears about yourself. Keep ever present before your mind's eye the goodness of the Heavenly Spouse Who sees, knows and weighs all our actions. You should not fear, because all your actions are directed to a good purpose. I can scarcely believe that you offend the Lord. On the contrary, I can see clearly that you are walking dutifully before Him, and that the storms which are now raging about you will finally turn to the glory of God, to your merit, and to the profit of many souls. I, even though unworthy, pray always to Our Lord for all your intentions. Be of good cheer, for the Heavenly Father will never permit the enemy to touch your spirit in these trials, nor that of your sister. I repeat: Courage, my sister! Be assured that God is with you! Why should you fear?"

San Giovanni Rotondo
August 23, 1918

J. M. J.

"My Dearest Daughter:

"May Jesus rule in your heart, and fill it to overflowing with His holy love. I am sorry not to be able to give an adequate answer to all the points you submitted in your last letter. For the last three days I have been sick, and I have just left my bed for a while in order to reply to your letter. You must forgive me if I do not write at length.

"In a general way I can assure you not to worry about the state of your soul, which is pleasing to God. But I cannot dispense you from meditation just because you seem to derive no profit from it. The sacred gift of prayer, my good daughter, is in the right hand of the Saviour, and He will begin to give it to you in the same measure in which you become free and empty of self, namely of the love of your body and of your own will, and in the measure that you become well-grounded in humility. Be patient and persevere in this holy exercise of meditation. Be satisfied to start taking short steps until the time when you have feet for running, and—still better—wings for flying. Be satisfied to submit to obedience, which is never a small thing for a soul that has chosen God for her portion. Be resigned, for the present, to remain as a little honeybee in the nest, for very soon you will become a mature working bee, able to produce honey. Humble yourself always, and lovingly, before God and men, because God speaks to him whose heart is truly humble in His presence, and He fills it with His gifts. I think that I am not mistaken in saying that the reason you do not make your meditation well, or do not always succeed in it, must be the following:

"You approach your meditation with uneasiness and with great anxiety, hoping to find something that will leave your soul contented and consoled. This is enough to prevent you from ever finding what you seek, and from applying your mind to the object of your meditation, all of which will leave your heart empty of affections. Remember, my daughter, that when we are searching with great anxiety for something that is lost, we may touch it with our hands and see it with our eyes a hundred times without being aware of it. The result of this vain and useless anxiety is a weariness of spirit and the inability of the mind to concentrate on the subject before it. From this, as from a natural cause, there follows a certain coldness and dullness of spirit, especially in its affective part. I know of no other remedy than this: set aside all anxiety, for it is the most treacherous betrayer where true virtue and devotion are concerned. It seems to inspire us for good works, but it is not so, because it soon causes us to grow discouraged. For a while it does make us run, but only to see us stumble. For this reason we must shun anxiety on every occasion, especially in time of prayer, as I have told you many times. In order to succeed better in this, it will be necessary to remember that all the graces and consolations of prayer are living waters that flow not from this earth but from heaven, and that no effort of ours can make them flow, even though we dispose ourselves for them with great diligence, and always with a humble and peaceful mind. We must keep our hearts open to heaven and expect this heavenly dew from there. Do not forget, my daughter, to take this thought with you when you go to pray, because with this you will come close to God and will place yourself in His presence for two main reasons: First, to render Him all the honor and worship we owe. This can be obtained without any spoken words, either on the part of God or on our part, because this obligation can be satisfied by the fact that we acknowledge Him to be our God and ourselves His humble creatures, bent before Him in spirit, awaiting His orders. Courtiers in great number appear many times in the presence of the king, not with the intention of talking with him or listening to him, but merely to be seen by him and to be recognized as his loyal servants. This manner of staying in the presence of God in order to profess with our will that we are His servants is a most holy and excellent practice, one involving great perfection.

"You may laugh at this, but I mean it.

"The second reason why we place ourselves in the presence of God during prayer is to talk to Him and to hear His voice by means of His inspiration and enlightenment. Ordinarily this is done with great joy, because it is a signal favor for us to talk to such a great Lord, Who, in answering, pours out a thousand balms and precious ointments upon us so as to give an immense peace to our souls. Now, my good daughter, one or the other of these two blessings can never fail you in your prayer. If you are able to speak to the Lord, speak to Him, praise Him, listen to Him. If you are unable to talk, because you are still inexpert in the ways of the spirit, remain before Him as a courtier and pay reverence to Him. He will notice you, appreciate your patience, accept your silence, and the next time He will satisfy you for He will take you by the hand, He will talk to you, and take you along many, many times promenading through His garden of prayer. Should this never come to pass (which is scarcely possible, because this loving Father cannot stand the sight of His creature in perpetual distress) be satisfied, because it is our duty to follow Him, remembering that it is already a great honor and favor for us to be tolerated in His presence. In this way you will not be too anxious to talk to Him because the opportunity of being near to Him is no less profitable, and probably it is even more so, even though it is less appealing to us. . . .

"The prayers for which you ask will never fail you, because I cannot forget for whom I had to make so many sacrifices, you whom I have borne to God in the extreme pain of my heart. I trust that in your charity you will not forget Him in your prayers Who carries the Cross for all. . . .

P. Pio, Cappuccino."[3]

San Giovanni Rotondo
May 7, 1919

To Fr. Angelo da Camerino
Republic of San Marino
"Very Esteemed Padre:

"May Jesus always rule as the supreme King in our hearts! May He comfort you in all the trials to which He is pleased to subject you, and may He make you worthy of the glory of the Blessed in heaven.

"I am supremely happy because the grace of God has offered me the pleasure to see your welcome and most precious writing, and I would be happier still if I could meet you personally.

"I shall not fail to pray for all your intentions. May God be pleased to accept the prayers I offer to Him. Do not fail to remember me in your own most worthy prayers. How can I express to you my appreciation and my gratitude for having

---

[3] We have included this letter, not only for its inspiring content but also for its historical interest. It was written less than a month before Padre Pio's stigmatization. The one which follows was written some seven months afterwards. The brevity of this latter note bears witness to the pain in the Padre's wounded right hand.

numbered me among the devotees of your renowned shrine? I shall try to prove my gratitude to you, in my humble way, before Jesus.

"May the grace of God guide and protect you in all things. . . .

Most devotedly in the Lord,
Padre Pio da Pietrelcina, Cappuccino."

SPIRITUAL ADVICE

By study we search for God, by meditation we find Him.

The life of a Christian is nothing but a constant struggle against self, and its beauty does not become manifest except at the price of suffering.

As long as you are afraid to commit sin, you will not sin.

Too much fear makes us act without love, too much confidence prevents us from seeing and dreading the danger we must face. Love tends towards its object and it is blind in its advance, it sees not; holy fear illumines love.

If you succeed in overcoming a temptation, this will have the same effect on your soul as lye has upon dirty linen.

If we are calm and patient we shall find not only ourselves but also our soul and God with it.

The devil has only one door by which to enter our soul—our will. There are no secret doors. There is no sin, as long as there is no free consent of the will. When the will had no part in it, there was no sin, only human weakness.

Have you observed a field of wheat at the time of the harvest? Some ears stand up above others that are bent. If you take the former in your hand, you will find that they are empty; the others, the humbler ones, are full of ripe grain. From this you will learn that vanity means emptiness.

All prayers are good when performed with a good intention and good will.

Prayer must be insistent, because insistence implies faith.

God fills the soul that empties itself of all else.

Every lie is the daughter of the devil.

Humility is truth, and truth is humility.

Prayer is the best weapon we possess, the key that opens the heart of God.

To fail against charity is to wound God in the pupil of His eye.

A good heart is always strong.

Love and fear must always be together. Fear without love becomes cowardice. Love without fear becomes presumption.

Where there is no obedience there is no virtue, where there is no virtue there is no good, where there is no good there is no love, where there is no love there is no God, and where there is no God there is no Paradise.

Humility and purity of life are wings that lift us up to God and almost deify us. Remember this: The evildoer who is ashamed to do evil is closer to God than the honest man who is ashamed to act honestly.

———————

Chapter Fifteen

The Voice of Charity

ON the evening of January 9, 1940, three "shipwrecked souls," friends and spiritual children of Padre Pio, were sitting with him in Cell Five in the Monastery of Our Lady of Grace. He was discussing the sufferings which afflict poor humanity at all times, but especially in time of war. From man's misery and suffering, he passed on to a more consoling subject—that of God's mercy and love for man, and of man's love for God.

"One single act of love on the part of man," he said, "one single act of charity, is so great in God's eyes that He could not repay it even with the immense gift of the entire Creation! Love is the spark of God in man's soul, it is the very essence of God personified in the Holy Spirit. To God we owe *all* our love, which, to be adequate, ought to be infinite. But this cannot be, because God alone is infinite. We must at least give our whole being to love, to charity. Our actions must be such that Our Lord may say to us 'I was hungry and you gave Me to eat; I was suffering and you cared for Me and comforted Me.'

"To carry out this ideal of Our Lord, we must be quite forgetful of self. Rising above selfishness, we must bow down to the sufferings and the wounds of our fellowmen. We must make them our own, knowing how to suffer with our brethren for the love of God. We must know how to instill hope into their hearts and bring back a smile to their lips, having restored a ray of light into their souls. Then we shall be offering God the

123

most beautiful, the most noble of prayers, because our prayer will have sprung from sacrifice. It will be the very essence of love, the unselfish gift of all that we are in body and soul. In every sick man there is Jesus in Person Who is suffering; in every poor man it is Jesus Himself Who is languishing; in every man who is both sick and poor, Jesus is doubly visible."

Eventually Padre Pio's long-cherished dream of building a large and up-to-date hospital in San Giovanni Rotondo became a reality. At first, of course, from a human point of view, the whole undertaking seemed utterly impracticable, "a crazy enterprise," as some called it. For the majestic structure had to be built some 2,400 feet above sea level, on a barren mountain slope, twenty-five miles away from Foggia, the nearest town of any importance.

Since there were no railways close at hand, it was also imperative that many workshops be provided. Hence, a kiln was built for making lime from stone dug out of the mountainside. Then apparatus was set up for the manufacture of cement slabs, artificial stone, marble, tiles, etc. Both water and electricity were absent and had to be provided for. But all these technical difficulties were as nothing compared to those of a financial nature.

At the conclusion of his talk to the three "shipwrecked souls" on that January night in 1940, Padre Pio produced from his pocket a small gold coin which had been given to him for his charities. Handing this to his friends, he said: "I wish to be the first to make a donation towards the hospital."

This, then, was the original capital for the Padre's cherished project. Divine Providence and Christian charity would have to supply the rest.

Gradually a few small contributions began to come in, followed by a large donation of one million three hundred thousand *lire* from a friend abroad, in pre-war currency. However, the shadow of World War II was ominously close, and on June 10 Mussolini plunged his country into the dreadful conflict.

This tragedy seemed to sweep away every hope for success, and now the three "shipwrecked souls" were at a complete loss. However, Padre Pio was praying, suffering and storming heaven for their mutual intention. He advised his friends to invest what funds they had collected in a landed estate. This proved to be an extremely wise investment, for very soon inflation was sweeping the country.

By 1943 American soldiers stationed at the air base of Foggia had discovered Padre Pio, and the Monastery of Our Lady of Grace became a popular place of pilgrimage. Soon the idea of the hospital was revived, and in October, 1946, it entered a new phase by becoming incorporated under an official title: "Home for the Relief of Suffering." Its statutes declared that the principal object of the hospital was "to receive any person who appeals for assistance and charity in the name of Christ."

By this time there were only four million *lire* on hand, in greatly devaluated post-war currency (about one-eightieth of the pre-war rate.) However, the board placed all its confidence in God, and work on the new building was begun on April 16, 1947. Despite the great need for funds, the founders imposed one rule upon themselves: not to ask anything of anyone, but to seek only the help of God.

In the fall of 1947, Barbara Ward of London went to San Giovanni Rotondo, urged by spiritual motives and perhaps also by her practical sense as an outstanding writer for *The Economist*. As a result of her visit, and without any request being made, 250 million *lire* of UNRRA funds were assigned to the new hospital with the sole stipulation that it bear the name of Fiorello La Guardia, the late Mayor of New York City.

A plaque on a wall outside the hospital expresses gratitude to the late Fiorello La Guardia of New York who was then Director General of the United Nations Relief and Rehabilitation Administration. The balance had to be collected lira by lira and dime by dime from all the many friends of Padre Pio. The main structure now had accommodations for three hundred and fifty beds, and rooms for about sixty nurses. Of course much remained to be done before Lady Charity could rule supreme over human suffering, but that happy day arrived only six years later.

The one who has been the most practical instrument of Divine Providence in the realization of all this work was Angelo Lupi of Pescara, a man of vision, a painter of renown, an architect, a real genius. Mention must also be made of Dr. Sanguinetti, Director of the Hospital, Dr. Kiswarday and Dr. Sanvico, who offered themselves to Padre Pio to carry out the plan and direct the work. These are the "shipwrecked souls" mentioned before.

On October 21, 1950, Padre Pio visited his cherished project and complimented all those who had contributed to its realization. He signed his name in the visitors' book and also inscribed the following:

"Having visited the whole building, I do not know what to admire more—the structure for its perfect harmony, or the kindness of Signor Lupi and of Dr. Sanguinetti. . . . Praise be to God and sincere thanks to our benefactors and to all who have contributed to the realization of this work of Christian charity. . . .

P. Pio da Pietrelcina.

10-21-1950, A.S. (Anno Santo: Holy Year)"

Padre Pio does not like the word "hospital," because it evokes ideas of loneliness, of pain, and death. He prefers to call his institution a house to relieve suffering, and his idea has prevailed. When we speak of it as a *hospital* we do so in order to simplify matters. The "hospital" has three hundred fifty beds and the following departments: Surgery, Medicine, Obstetrics, Gynecology, Cardiology, Orthopedy, and Pediatry. The clinic offers these services: surgical, medical, obstetrical, gynecological, pediatric, orthopedic, as well as for eyes, ears, and mouth. The hospital has a first aid office open day and night; it even has a helicopter landing place on the roof for emergency patients.

May 5, 1956, was the official date for the opening and inauguration of the *Casa Sollievo della Sofferenza,* an event which attracted world wide attention. A large group of the foremost heart specialists in the world attended the inauguration of the new hospital and consecrated its name to science and research with a symposium on coronary diseases, held in the lecture hall of this new institution, while Padre Pio consecrated it to Christian charity and love. Among the specialists present were Dr. Paul Dudley White of Boston and Dr. O. H. Wangensteen of Minneapolis. Others came from Rome, Milan, Bologna, Florence, Genoa; from London, Brussels, Paris, Stockholm, Barcelona, and from Switzerland, Argentina and other lands. All these Doctors, with some members of their families were, later on, received in audience by the Holy Father in Rome. In the greatly admired allocution given by the Holy Father to this group of specialists, reference was made to the special nature and scope of the new institution inspired by Padre Pio, as a place that is intended to introduce a new concept in the care of the sick, a concept which is both humane and supernatural.

Before leaving the new hospital this distinguished group of specialists went to the humble Monastery of Our Lady of Grace to express their admiration to Padre Pio for the marvelous work he had created. "I return to America," said Dr. Paul Dudley

White, "profoundly impressed with Padre Pio's work. This hospital, more than any other in the world, seems to me best suited to study the relations that exist between the mind and sickness. Here, more than anywhere else, the study of psychosomatic illness can progress." "Too bad," said Dr. Wangersteen of Minneapolis, "that there is only one Padre Pio in the world." The same feelings were expressed by this Doctor to the Holy Father at the end of the above mentioned audience in Rome. The Holy Father replied: "May God send us many more of such good and holy priests!" With great emotion, Dr. Lian of Paris bowed to Padre Pio and with great respect said: "I bring to Padre Pio the most profound admiration of Paris and of France." Speaking in the name of the European Society of Cardiology, whose president he was, Dr. G. Nylin of Stockholm said: "We bow respectfully before Padre Pio, author of such a magnificent act of charity. With his unshaken faith, his love for mankind, Padre Pio gives us a splendid example of abnegation in the service of our fellow men. This hospital is a tangible proof of the good Samaritan. With all our heart we wish that God may bless the noble and charitable intentions of Padre Pio." Mortified by all these and many other manifestations of esteem, Padre Pio replied with only a few words: "Bring God to all those who are sick, this will help them more than any other remedy. If you do not bring love to the sickbed, I do not think that medicines will do much good." And with these words he blessed them all and then slowly retired to the solitude of his cell to suffer and to pray. It was because he saw Christ himself in his suffering brother that he wanted his hospital to look almost like a royal palace: "In every sick man there is Jesus Himself Who is suffering," he had told those three shipwrecked souls one day, "in every poor man it is Jesus Himself Who is languishing; in every man who is both sick and poor, Jesus is doubly present." This was and remains the charter of the new hospital.

The fifth of May, the date of the official opening, was chosen for a special reason; on that day, the feast of St. Pius V, Padre Pio celebrates his name's day, that is, his feast day. It was proper that this great monument of Christian charity, conceived by his selfless mind and his loving heart, should be connected with his name and that the joy of this event should add to the joy of his own feast day.

Early that morning, May 5, 1956, a crowd of about fifteen thousand people had gathered on the esplanade in front of the new hospital in order to assist at the inaugural Mass celebrated by Padre Pio on a portable altar in front of the majestic structure. At seven o'clock that morning Padre Pio appeared in his priestly vestments preceded by a lay Brother who carried the chalice for the Mass, a necessary precaution in view of the fact that the deep wounds in Padre Pio's hands do not give him a firm grip on the sacred vessel. In perfect silence and deep devotion the large audience followed the mystical development of the Sacrifice of the Mass. Immediately after Consecration the three hundred flags—including the American—atop the new structure began to quiver and to flutter joyously as if announcing the coming of the Spirit, the Spirit of Charity. Many celebrities were present at Mass; both the Italian Government and Senate were represented; local authorities, from Foggia and San Giovanni Rotondo, were there. Before the Mass came to a close, Cardinal Giacomo Lercaro of Bologna arrived at the Hospital for the inauguration.

Among those many thousands assisting at Padre Pio's Mass that morning there was particularly one man who attracted the attention of all present. It was noticed that this man was in tears most of the time during Mass, and at the end of it he went to Padre Pio, kissed his hands and broke down crying. His name is Dr. Carlo Kisvarday, the pharmacist of the *Casa Sollievo della Sofferenza*, the only survivor of the original trio, the three ship-wrecked souls, to whom Padre Pio had entrusted his great plan and his hopes for the new hospital. They worked together in the most selfless manner and in the face of enormous difficulties and oppositions. The other two, Dr. Guglielmo Sanguinetti, and Dr. Mario Sanvico went to their reward without seeing the crowning glory of this inaugural day; the first died in 1954, the other in 1955.

His Holiness Pope Pius XII sent his Apostolic Blessing with a message read by the Superior General of the Capuchins at the beginning of the inaugural addresses. In his message the Holy Father referred to the new hospital as "a work inspired by a profound sense of charity." The traditional cutting of the ribbon was performed jointly by His Eminence Card. Lercaro and Padre Pio. On this occasion His Eminence pronounced some very inspiring words: "It is superfluous for us to address you in a place where things themselves talk far more eloquently... I have been reminded of those words of our sacred liturgy: 'Where charity and love dwell, God is there.' It is equally true that where God is, there charity and love are found together . . . Have you not noticed it here in San Giovanni Rotondo? Yes, the whole world has noticed it! God is here! manifestly, therefore, charity and love dwell here."

With his customary simplicity and profound humility, Padre Pio said: "Divine Providence, with your very kind assistance, has produced this work which I now present to you. Admire it and join me in praising Our Almighty God . . ."

When Charity speaks, as it does at the Casa Sollievo della Sofferenza, it is God that speaks, because God is Charity.

Padre Pio saying Mass the morning
of the inauguration of the House for
the Relief of Suffering, May 5, 1956.

VIEW OF THE CITY ON A MOUNTAIN, IN THE CENTER, AT LEFT: THE NEW AND OLD CHURCH AND MONASTERY OF OUR LADY OF GRACE, AT RIGHT THE ENLARGED HOUSE FOR THE RELIEF OF SUFFERING IN 1963.

Chapter Sixteen

The City on a Mountain

P adre Pio's City on a Mountain grew first around the old church and monastery of Our Lady of Grace and then around the modern and stately hospital which Padre Pio wanted.

Christ, our Blessed Savior, said of himself: "If I be lifted up from the earth, will draw all things to myself." The Evangelist adds these words of explanation: "now he said this signifying by what death he was to die." John 12:32f. The lifting up of Christ was meant here not of his glorious Ascension to heaven after his triumphant Resurrection, but of the lifting up of the cross on which he was nailed on Calvary and on which he was to die the infamous death of a malefactor, thereby paying to God the price of redemption for sinful humanity.

When on September 20, 1918, Padre Pio received the stigmata in the old monastery church on Mt. Gargano, he was actually crucified mystically, nailed to an invisible cross and lifted up for the entire world and the people of this generation to see. He was not to die soon, putting an end to the atrocious pains of his five wounds, some three hours later, like Christ, or after two years, like Francis of Assisi, Padre Pio's own master and model, but the suffering and the bleeding of his crucifixion was to last and continue unbroken for many long years till old age. He is still cruicified, today, in the year of Our Lord, March 13, 1965, while we are writing this. But, today, the City on a Mountain, which for years has resembled Calvary, begins to assume the resemblance of the beauty and glory of Mt. Tabor. Only one year after the official opening of the *House for the Relief of Suffering,* this great work of faith and charity had already reached such perfection and stability in its management and such favor and admiration with the people that the Holy Father Pius XII saw the time ripe to provide for the future of the hospital giving a stable juridical form to its administration. On the occasion of Padre Pio's birthday, on May 5, 1957, he received from the Pope, through the Secretary of State, a precious and important document wherein he was appointed Director for life of the *Franciscan Third Order of Our Lady of Grace* which had been previously appointed administrator of the *House for the Relief of Suffering.* Padre Pio was given the privilege of personally guiding and directing the development of the Hospital, assisted by experts he was permitted to choose among the members of the same Third Order. At the same time the Holy See dispensed Padre Pio of the religious vow of Poverty for practical reasons of administration, which did not change at all his deep spirit of poverty. May the fifth has been always a feast day for Padre Pio and his many spiritual sons and daughters everywhere, but on this day, in 1957, he had the great satisfaction of being able to address his spiritual friends with the following inspired words: "May Our Lord be blessed! The work whose beginning you witnessed a year ago today, is now completing its first year of existence. The *House for the Relief of Suffering* has opened its arms to thousands of persons with sick bodies and souls, thus extending the benefits of your charity to everyone who has been recovered here this year, without any distinction between the richest and the poorest, ministering to everyone the means wherewith you endowed it, in a very generous measure. God has warmed up with His warm rays of love the seeds you have planted. From its very beginning, this work was obliged to ask for help from the charity of generous persons in order to attain a juridical systematization and a stable settlement. To all of them I do here express my deepest gratitude. Today, by disposition of Our Holy Father, this Work has attained its autonomy. The august Pontiff with his provident and sollicitous bounty has graciously disposed that the Work should have a juridical adjustment corresponding to its own special aims. . . .

"Here, at the *House for the Relief of Suffering,* we have always offered prayers assiduously for the august and venerable person of the Vicar of Christ. By this munificent act, the *House for the Relief of Suffering* feels bound by even greater duties of gratitude to Pope Pius XII who has watched over its first signs of life. Today, we enter upon the second part of our way when the Work must recommend itself once more to your generosity so that it may become a Hospital City, technically adequate to the highest clinical exigencies. The Home must increase its present number of beds. Two new Homes must be added to this one. A Home for women, and one for men, where their tired and weary bodies and spirits may come to Our Lord and find their rest. An intercontinental center of studies shall assist doctors and nurses to integrate and perfect their professional culture and their Christian formation.

"We must complete the systematization of this Work that it may become a temple of prayer and of science, where mankind can find itself in Jesus Crucified, as one fold and one shepherd. The children of this Work who in every part of the world come together to pray in common according to the spirit of our seraphic father St. Francis, and in line with the directives and the intentions of the Pope, must find here the common home of their groups; the priests shall find here their own Cenacle; the men, the religious women shall find here houses where they can develop even more their spiritual formation and their ascent to God, so that in faith, detachment, and self-immolation they may live the love of God which is the consummation of Christian perfection.

"To his activity of a Divine Teacher, Jesus added the activity of a healing physician. He is the author of life who died once but lives and reigns eternally. If this Work were merely a relief for sick bodies it would be no more than a model Clinic, but with your means extraordinarily generous, your charity has willed and urged that it should become an efficient appeal to the love of God by means of the appeal of charity itself.

"The suffering patient must live in himself the love of God by a wise acceptance of his pains and a serene meditation of his destiny for God. Here the love of God must be strengthened in the spirit of every patient through his love for Jesus Crucified. Here patients, physicians, priests shall be reservoirs of love which will communicate itself much easier to others, the more abundant it is found in one of them . . . ."

The triumphs of charity here illustrated by Padre Pio and made evident in the *House for the Relief of Suffering,* were also triumphs of generosity and patience. The generosity manifested itself from the time the idea of a hospital was launched by Padre Pio, as we explained in chapter fifteen of this book, where the many reasons for great patience were also mentioned, chief among them the second World War. Not many months ago, an interesting newspaper report from Rome, Italy, seems to confirm both generosity and patience as necessary elements in the building up of the City on a Mountain. "Rome's civil tribunal, has ruled, that Padre Pio of Pietrelcina, the stigmatic Capuchin priest is now heir to a real estate that is valued at more than three million dollars, $3,000,000. This estate had been willed to him, as the representative of the House for the Relief of Suffering, at San Giovanni Rotondo, by Dr. Mario de Giacomo. The will stipulated that in case Padre Pio abandoned his plan to build a hospital or he refused the inheritance, the property should go to the state hospitals in Naples. The state hospitals contested the will in 1952, on the grounds that at the time of the doctor's death there was still no hospital belonging to Padre Pio. As we have seen, the hospital was completed and opened in May, 1956.

Note: Father Pio's personal persecutions and sufferings increased during Vatican Council II, although literally hundreds of Bishops took advantage of the proximity of Father Pio to visit him during these years. Many went incognito. One Vatican official in particular was responsible for these great trials and when Pope Paul was elected, a consoling letter from the Pope put an end to them. However the last years of Padre Pio were years exactly like all that had gone before. He lived to carry the burdens of all who asked, and to increase holiness in all who approached. He was the twentieth century's APOSTLE OF HOLINESS.

THE HOME FOR THE RELIEF OF SUFFERING.

Chapter Seventeen

The Mass of Padre Pio in Pictures

IT is only during Mass that Padre Pio takes off the half gloves which cover the stigmata of his hands. Even then, by pulling down the sleeves of the alb, he manages to hide the holy marks, especially at the beginning of Mass. The large dark spot seen on his hands in the photographs is dried blood. It is very red in the center, where it is still fresh and oozing constantly. These spots are all that people can see of Padre Pio's stigmata, and to affirm that one has been to San Giovanni Rotondo and "has studied them at first hand," is a gross misstatement.

We have been assured authoritatively that Padre Pio was ordered to wear gloves by his Superior General. He may not show his wounds to anyone at any time, and not even the local or Provincial Superior may dispense from this prohibition.

During the Holy Year of 1950, and the Vatican Council II, many Bishops visited Padre Pio. One of them, the Vicar Apostolic of Iceland, asked the Padre if he might not see the wounds in his hands. Padre Pio replied that this was absolutely forbidden by his superiors.

Padre Pio did not pose for the following pictures, nor was he aware that they were being taken. As anyone can see, they are not pictures of the same Mass, the vestments differing in color and appearance. Nevertheless, they show with what great love and devotion the Padre offers the Holy Sacrifice.

PRAYERS AT THE FOOT OF THE ALTAR

"I will go to the Altar of God,
   To God Who is the joy of my youth. . . ."

THE COLLECT
The stigma on the back of his right hand becomes visible.

THE OFFERTORY
"Accept, O Holy Father, Almighty and Eternal God, this Immaculate Host. . . ."

POURING WINE AND WATER IN THE CHALICE

"O God . . . grant that through the mystery of this water and wine we may be made partakers of His Divinity, Who has deigned to become partaker of our humanity, Jesus Christ, Thy Son, Our Lord. . . ."

141

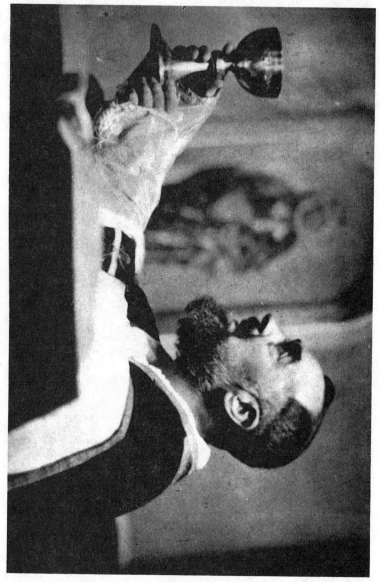

OFFERING THE CHALICE

"We offer unto Thee, O Lord, the Chalice of salvation. . . . ."

142

THE ORATE FRATRES

"Brethren, pray that my sacrifice and yours may become acceptable to God the Father Almighty."

CONSECRATION OF THE BREAD—I

"The day before He suffered, took bread into His Holy and
venerable hands . . . blessed it. . . ."

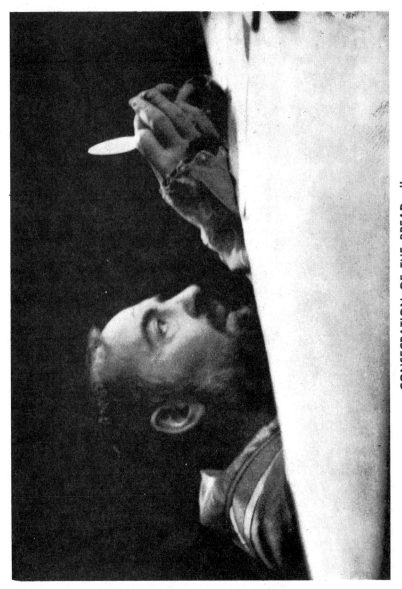

CONSECRATION OF THE BREAD—II
Kneeling to adore the consecrated Host.

145

CONSECRATION OF THE BREAD—III
Elevation of the Sacred Host.

ELEVATION OF THE CHALICE
He still manages to keep the stigmata covered.

146

OUR FATHER WHO ART IN HEAVEN . . .
The blood of the stigmata surrounds the base of the little finger
of the right hand.

147

THE COMMUNION OF THE PRIEST—I

"Domine non sum dignus: Lord I am not worthy. . . ."

THE COMMUNION OF THE PRIEST—II

"I will take the Chalice of salvation, and I will call upon the
Name of the Lord. . . ."
The Blood of the Saviour **in** the chalice,
his own blood **on** the chalice.

149

COMMUNION OF THE FAITHFUL
  "Ecce Agnus Dei...."

THE FINAL BLESSING
"May God Almighty bless you...."

THE BLESSING
  "The Father, the Son, and the Holy Ghost. . . ."

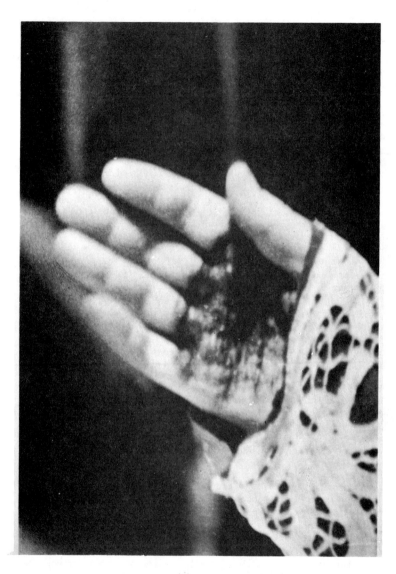

PADRE PIO'S RIGHT HAND
"The Lord be with you!"

DEAR LORD, MY FATHER

Let me dwell on the amazing truth that You love me. Let me ponder on this overwhelming revelation. Let me understand that because You love me as a Father loves his child, You constantly invite me to share the joy of your eternal kingdom.

May I always hear Your call, Father; and let me accept the fact that my brief span of life on earth is Your gift of freedom. A time to choose the ultimate destiny of my soul, that invisible jewel linked in Your glorious chain of eternity.

How carelessly we treat Your divine gift of life. How seldom do we invite You to enter our soul to let it warm itself in the bright light of Your love. Instead, we leave it to agonize under a dark mantle of indifference.

It has been ever thus, Father, throughout the ages. And because Your children turned a deaf ear to Your call, because we thought Your commands were inhuman, You sent us Your most precious gift of all, Your only Son, Jesus. He came to show us that Your laws were not those of a tyrannical Father, but guidelines that culminate in but a single request: To Love. To love You, Father, and to love all of humanity because all of us share the right to Your divine legacy.

And Jesus came and dwelt among us. And because He desired our souls as a gift-offering to You, Father, He gave His life for the love of us.

Jesus could have died in a thousand different ways. But He chose to be nailed to a wooden cross. He chose a cross as the symbol for our eternal salvation. The cross to identify the children of God. The cross to brandish as a token of love, and a shield to overcome all evil.

Lord, throughout the centuries You have tried to waken us from our indolent statue by showing that the Cross is the true sign of our redemption, and that it is only through the crucified Jesus that we can enter Your kingdom. You have shown it in visions to warriors and saints, to emperors as well as to the hermit. And most of all You have shown it in wounds visibly imprinted as living stigmatas on many of Your sons and daughters. Among the bearers You chose St. Francis of Assisi, St. Theresa of Avila and, in our own time, a humble Capuchin, Padre Pio of Pietrelcina.

Through these saintly messengers You are telling us, Father, to take the holy cross and make it the real symbol of our alliance with Christ. For it is true that the cross has disappeared or has been put to one side, even in holy places. It has been replaced by banners and flags and other artifacts that are perhaps pleasing to the eye but not the soul. And when the cross is absent, the forces of evil take over and reign in Your stead.

You are reminding us once again through Padre Pio to take the Cross and return it to its rightful place as the Blazon of Christianity.

Let it be so, Father. Let me wear the Cross as a follower of Your Son, Jesus Christ. Let it remind me of Your constant love and become the divine symbol of my redemption, indelibly marking me with the sign of charity, joy and peace, so that I may be counted among Your children for all eternity.